60
Quick
Baby
Blankets

60 Quick Baby Blankets

CUTE & CUDDLY KNITS IN 220 SUPERWASH® AND 128 SUPERWASH® FROM CASCADE YARNS

THE EDITORS OF SIXTH&SPRING BOOKS

sixth&springbooks NEW YORK

sixth&springbooks

161 Avenue of the Americas, New York, NY 10013
sixthandspringbooks.com

Editorial Director
JOY AQUILINO

Developmental Editor
LISA SILVERMAN

Art Director
DIANE LAMPHRON

Yarn Coordinator
CHRISTINA BEHNKE

Editorial Assistant
JOHANNA LEVY

Instructions Editors
CARLA SCOTT
RENEE LORION
STEPHANIE MRSE
AMY POLCYN
SANDI PROSSER
JUDY SLOAN
LORI STEINBERG

Instructions Proofreaders
STEPHANIE MRSE
JUDY SLOAN

Technical Illustrator
ULI MONCH

Photography
JACK DEUTSCH

Front Cover Photography
MARCUS TIULLIS

....

Vice President
TRISHA MALCOLM

Publisher
CAROLINE KILMER

Creative Director
JOE VIOR

Production Manager
DAVID JOINNIDES

President
ART JOINNIDES

ISBN 978-1-936096-46-6

Manufactured in China
3 5 7 9 10 8 6 4 2
First Edition

CASCADE YARNS
DISTRIBUTOR OF FINE YARN

cascadeyarns.com

contents

Check It Out!

Turn to the inside back cover to find abbreviations, an explanation of skill levels, illustrations of embroidery stitches, and even a handy ruler!

bundle up your bundle of joy

Following the success of the 60 Quick Knits series, especially *60 Quick Baby Knits* and *60 More Quick Baby Knits*, we are proud to present *60 Quick Baby Blankets*—a collection of beautiful blankets to make and to give.

Knitters will love the variety of styles, techniques, shapes, and sizes—and so will parents and babies! All the blankets in this book were knit in Cascade 220 Superwash or Cascade 128 Superwash, its bulkier cousin. Both are perfect yarns for baby blankets: soft, durable, washable, and affordable, with an unmatchable range of colors, from pastels to vibrant brights.

Whether you're knitting for your own little one or a friend's new arrival, you'll find something to suit every nursery here—from modern to traditional, boyish to feminine—including bold, graphic stripes and color blocks, cozy cables and textures, adorable intarsia animals, precious lace motifs, and much more! With the dozens of projects in this book, you'll never have to look for the perfect gift for a new baby again.

 To locate retailers that carry 220 Superwash and 128 Superwash, visit cascadeyarns.com.

Tickled Pink

A multitude of pinks forms the bricks and cream is the mortar in this sweet slip-stitch afghan.

DESIGNED BY LISA SILVERMAN

Knitted Measurements
Approx 33" x 32"/83.5cm x 81cm

Materials
■ 2 3½oz/100g balls (each approx 220yd/200m) of Cascade Yarns *220 Superwash* (superwash wool) in #910A winter white (A)

■ 1 ball each in #1940 peach (B), #834 strawberry pink (C), #903 flamingo pink (D), and #838 rose petal (E)

■ Size 7 (4.5mm) circular needle, 32"/80cm long, *or size to obtain gauge*

Blanket
With A, cast on 143 sts.
Row 1 (RS) Knit.
Row 2 *K5, k1 wrapping yarn 3 times around needle; rep from * to last 5 sts, end k5.
Row 3 Join B, *k5, sl 1 wyib, dropping extra wraps; rep from * to last 5 sts, end k5.

Row 4 Purl, slipping A sts wyif.
Rows 5 and 6 Rep rows 3 and 4 twice more.
Row 7 With A, knit.
Row 8 With A, k2, *k1 wrapping 3 times around needle, k5; rep from * to last 3 sts, end k1 with 3 wraps, k2.
Row 9 Join C, *k5, sl 1 wyib, dropping extra wraps; rep from * to last 5 sts, end k5.
Row 10 Purl, slipping A sts wyif.
Rows 11 and 12 Rep rows 9 and 10 twice more.
Row 13 With A, knit.
Row 14 With A, k2, *k1 wrapping 3 times around needle, k5; rep from * to last 3 sts, end k1 with 3 wraps, k2.
Row 15 Join D, *k5, sl 1 wyib, dropping extra wraps; rep from * to last 5 sts, end k5.
Row 16 Purl, slipping A wyif.
Rows 17 and 18 Rep rows 15 and 16 twice more.
Row 19 With A, knit.
Row 20 With A, k2, *k1 wrapping 3 times around needle, k5; rep from * to last 3 sts, end k1 with 3 wraps, k2.
Row 21 Join E, *k5, sl 1 wyib, dropping extra wraps; rep from * to last 5 sts, end k5.
Row 22 Purl, slipping A wyif.

Rows 23 and 24 Rep rows 21 and 22 twice more.
Row 25 With A, knit.
Row 26 With A, k2, *k1 wrapping 3 times around needle, k5; rep from * to last 3 sts, end k1 with 3 wraps, k2.
Rep rows 1–26 six times more. Rep rows 1–12 once more.

BORDER
Join A, knit 1 row, dec 10 sts evenly across row—133 sts.
Work 3 more rows in garter st (k every row). Bind off.
With A, pick up 136 sts along left side of blanket. Knit 4 rows garter st. Bind off.
With A, pick up 133 sts along bottom of blanket. Knit 4 rows garter st. Bind off.
With A, pick up 136 sts along right side of blanket. Knit 4 rows garter st. Bind off.

Finishing
Weave in ends. Block lightly to measurements. ■

Gauges
19 sts and 28 rows to 4"/10cm over St st using size 7 (4.5mm) circular needle.
17 sts and 30 rows to 4"/10cm over pat st using size 7 (4.5mm) circular needle. *Take time to check gauges.*

Graphically Gray

A burst of orange at the border is the perfect finishing touch for neutral chevron stripes.

DESIGNED BY WILMA PEERS

Knitted Measurements
Approx 28"x 36"/71cm x 91.5cm

Materials
- 2 3.5oz/100g balls (each approx 220yd/201m) Cascade Yarns *220 Superwash* (superwash wool) each in #871 white (A) and #874 ridge rock (B)
- 1 ball in #825 orange (C)
- One size 9 (5.5mm) circular needle, 32"/80cm long, *or size to obtain gauge*
- One size G/6 (4mm) crochet hook
- Stitch holders

Note
Blanket is worked back and forth in rows. Circular needle is used to accommodate large number of sts—do not join.

Stitch Glossary
LIL (lifted increase left) Insert LH needle into the left leg of the previous st from back to front, two rows below, and knit—1 st inc.

LIR (lifted increase right) Insert RH needle into the right leg of the next st from front to back, one row below, and knit—1 st inc.

Stripe Sequence
[6 rows A, 6 rows B] 16 times, 6 rows A.

Blanket
With size 9 (5.5mm) circular needle and A, cast on 160 sts. Purl 1 row (WS). Following stripe sequence, proceed in pat as follows:

Row 1 (RS) K3, [LIL, k10, ssk, k2tog, k10, LIR, k2] 6 times, k1.
Row 2 Purl.
Repeat last 2 rows for chevron pat.
Cont in pat to end of stripe sequence, end with a WS row. Bind off all sts knitwise.

TOP TRIANGULAR INSERTS
Start at upper right-hand corner, with right side facing and B, pick up and k 27 sts evenly along edge of first chevron. Turn.
*Row 1 (WS) P17, turn.
Row 2 Sl 1, k10, turn.
Row 3 Sl 1, p14, turn.
Row 4 Sl 1, k17, turn.
Row 5 Sl 1, p20, turn.
Row 6 Sl 1, k23, turn.
Row 7 Sl 1, p26, turn. Break yarn and leave sts on holder.
With right side facing and A, pick up and k 27 sts evenly along edge of next chevron. Turn.******
Repeat from * to ** until all chevrons have been worked—162 sts.
Next row (WS) Purl across all sts. Bind off.

BOTTOM TRIANGULAR INSERTS
Work as for top triangular inserts, creating five triangles between chevrons.

BOTTOM CORNER TRIANGLES
Turn blanket so bottom edge is at top. With right side facing and B, pick up and k5 sts beginning at top right corner (along half chevron in A). Turn.
Row 1 (WS) Sl 1, p to end.
Row 2 Sl 1, k4, pick up and k3 from chevron edge. Turn.
Row 3 Sl 1, p to end.
Row 4 Sl 1, k7, pick up and k3 from chevron edge. Turn.
Row 5 Sl 1, p to end.
Row 6 Sl 1, k10, pick up and k3 from chevron edge, reaching point. Turn.
Row 7 Sl 1, p to end. Bind off.
Rep for corner at left, reversing shaping.

Finishing
Block gently.

CROCHET EDGING
With crochet hook, right side facing, and 2 strands of C held together throughout, work 1 rnd single crochet around outer edge of blanket, working 2 sc into each corner. Join with a slip st to first sc, ch1. Work 1 round reverse single crochet. Join with a slip st to first st. Fasten off. ■

Gauge
23 sts and 22 rows to 4"/10cm over chevron pattern using size 9 (5.5mm) needles. *Take time to check gauge.*

Criss-Cross Coverlet

A repeating pattern of crossed cables stands out against a background of stockinette and garter bands.

DESIGNED BY TANIS GRAY

Finished measurements
Approx 34½" x 36"/87.5cm x 91.5cm after blocking

Materials
■ 5 3½oz/100g hanks (each approx 128yd/117m) of Cascade Yarns *128 Superwash* (superwash merino) in #905 celery

■ Size 11 (8mm) circular needle, 32"/80cm long, *or size to obtain gauge*

■ Cable needle (cn)

Stitch Glossary
4-st RC Sl 2 sts to cn and hold to back, k2, k2 from cn.

3-st RC Sl 1 st to cn and hold to back, k2, k1 from cn.

3-st LC Sl 2 to cn and hold to front, k1, k2 from cn.

Note
Blanket is worked in rows. Circular needle is used to accommodate large number of sts—do not join.

Blanket
Cast on 103 sts. Work in garter st (k every row) for 4 rows.

Next row (RS) Work row 1 of chart to rep line, work 9-st rep 11 times across, work to end of chart.
Cont to work chart in this manner through row 12. Rep rows 1–12 ten times more.
Work 4 rows of garter st.
Bind off.

Finishing
Weave in ends. Block lightly to measurements. ■

Stitch Key

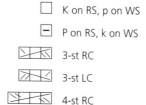

☐	K on RS, p on WS
⊟	P on RS, k on WS
	3-st RC
	3-st LC
	4-st RC

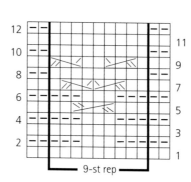

9-st rep

Gauge
12 sts and 14 rows after blocking to 4"/10cm over chart pat using size 11 (8mm) needles.
Take time to check gauge.

Monster Mash

No one told these monsters they were supposed to be scary!
Their playful smiles will put a smile on baby's face, too.

DESIGNED BY SUSAN B. ANDERSON

Knitted Measurements
Approx 32" x 33.5"/81cm x 85cm

Materials
■ 6 3½oz/100g hanks (each approx 128yd/117m) of Cascade Yarns *128 Superwash* (merino wool) in #896 blue horizon (A)

■ 1 hank each of #802 green apple (B), #815 black (C), #817 ecru (D), and #820 lemon (E)

■ Two size 10 (6mm) circular needles, 24"/61cm and 40"/101.5cm long, *or size to obtain gauge*

■ Stitch markers

■ Bobbins (optional)

Notes
1) The intarsia blocks are worked by cutting long lengths of the yarn that is left hanging at the back while working, and weaving into the wrong side at the end.
2) Remember to twist the yarn at the back when changing colors to prevent any gaps. The different colors can be cut in long lengths and left as is, or wound onto bobbins.
3) For the embroidery detail, weave in all ends to the wrong side as neatly as possible and trim.
4) One block is turned upside-down in the blanket to look as if the monster is doing a handstand. Other blocks have monsters jumping, waving, and dancing. Be creative and add some motion to your monsters. Don't be afraid of going into the border with your monster limbs.

Blanket
PLAIN BLOCK (MAKE 4)
With A and shorter circular needle, cast on 38 sts.
Knit 6 rows.

STOCKINETTE STITCH SECTION
Row 1 Knit.
Row 2 K3, p to last 3 sts, k3.

Rep rows 1 and 2 27 more times or until a total of 56 rows of the St st section have been worked.
Knit 6 rows.
Bind off, leaving a long tail for seaming.

MONSTER BLOCK (MAKE 5)
Beg the same as for the plain block, then work 16 rows of the St st section.
Beg chart as foll:
Row 1 Work the first 11 sts of the row as established, pm, work row 1 of chart, pm, work the last 11 sts of the row.
Cont working through row 26 of the chart, working first and last 11 stitches as set.
Work 16 rows of the St st section.
Knit 6 rows.
Bind off, leaving a long tail for seaming.

EMBROIDERY
Pupil With a cut length of C placed on a yarn needle, duplicate stitch 4 sts, two sts on the bottom and two sts directly above, on each eyeball in different places so the eyes are looking different ways.

Gauge
14 sts and 22 rows = 4"/10cm over St st using size 10 (6mm) circular needle.
Take time to check gauge.

Monster Mash

Mouth With a cut length of C placed on a yarn needle, make a smile using the split st. Place the smiles on different parts of the body to create different expressions.

Arms, legs, hands, and feet With a cut length of C placed on a yarn needle, use the split stitch to make the arms and legs. At the end of each leg and arm use the split stitch to outline a round foot or hand. Fill in the foot or hand using the satin stitch.

Hair With a cut length of C placed on a yarn needle, make 3 short hairs on top of each head (each hair a single strand of yarn). Length should vary between 3 and 7 sts above head.

Outline With a cut length of E placed on a yarn needle, use chain stitch to outline the body of the monster.

Finishing

Steam block squares. Lay out the completed blocks as desired. Seam the blocks into rows, then seam the rows into the final blanket.

BORDER

With longer circular needle, RS facing you, and D, beg at the lower left corner of the blanket, pick up 114 sts along the bottom edge, pm, pick up 1 st in the corner, pm, pick up 105 sts along the side, pm, pick up 1 st in the corner, pm, pick up 114 sts along the top edge, pm, pick up 1 st in the corner, pm, pick up 105 sts along the side, pm, pick up 1 st in the corner, pm. Place marker at beg of rnd—442 sts.

Work in the rnd as foll:
Purl 1 rnd. Switch to E.
Rnd 1 *K to marker, cast on 1 using backward lp method, k1, cast on 1; rep from * 3 more times—450 sts.
Rnd 2 Purl.
Switch to B and rep rnds 1 and 2—458 sts. With A, bind off.

Weave in ends. Block lightly to measurements. ∎

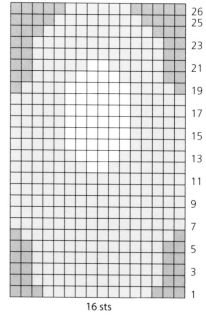

16 sts

Color Key

☐ Green Apple (B)

▨ Blue Horizon (A)

☐ Ecru (D)

Playing Checkers

Add a pastel pop of color to the nursery with this garter-stitch checkerboard pattern.

DESIGNED BY ELIZABETH NIELDS

Knitted Measurements
Approx 33.5"/85cm square

Materials
- 4 3.5"oz/100g hanks (each approx. 128yd/117m) of Cascade Yarns *128 Superwash* (merino wool) in #817 ecru (MC)
- 2 hanks in #1979 lilac mist (A)
- 3 hanks in #850 lime sherbet (B)
- One pair size 10 (6mm) needles *or size to obtain gauge*
- One size 10 (6mm) circular needle, 60"/150cm long
- Stitch holders
- Stitch markers

Notes
1) As you work the corners, turn the blanket so that the side you are working on is facing up (toward you).
2) When working mitered squares, always pick up sts with RS facing.

Stitch Glossary
KF&B Knit into front and back of stitch.

Mitered Square
Row 1 and all WS rows Knit.
Row 2 K22, S2KP, k22.
Row 4 K21, S2KP, k21.
Rows 6–44 Cont in this manner until 3 sts rem.
Row 46 S2KP.
Cut yarn, pull tail through lp on needle.

Blanket
CENTER STRIP
With size 10 (6mm) straight needles, waste yarn, and MC, cast on 23 sts using a provisional cast-on. Knit 46 rows. *Cut MC, knit 46 rows with A, cut A, knit 46 rows with MC; repeat from * once more—5 blocks. Place sts onto holder. Cut MC.

RIGHT SIDE STRIP
Holding center strip sideways, with A, pick up 23 sts along right side of MC center square. Knit 46 rows. Cut A, knit 46 rows with MC. Cut MC. Place all sts onto a holder.

LEFT SIDE STRIP
Holding center strip sideways, with A, pick up 23 sts along left side of MC center square. Knit 46 rows. Cut A, knit 46 rows with MC. Cut MC. Place all sts onto a holder.

UPPER RIGHT CORNER
With MC, beg with right side strip, pick up 23 sts from top edge of A block, pick up 1 st in corner, pick up 23 sts along right edge of upper part of center strip A block. Work mitered square.
With B, pick up 23 sts along top edge of MC block of right side strip, pick up 1 st in corner, pick up 23 sts along right edge of MC mitered square. Work mitered square.

Gauges
15 sts and 20 rows to 4"/10cm over St st using size 10 (6mm) needles.
15 sts and 32 rows to 4"/10cm over mitered square pat using size 10 (6mm) needles). *Take time to check gauges.*

Playing Checkers

With B, pick up 23 sts along top edge of MC mitered square, pick up 1 st in corner, pick up 23 sts along right edge of upper part of center strip MC block. Work mitered square. With MC, pick up 23 sts along top edge of first B mitered square, pick up 1 st in corner, pick up 23 sts along right edge of second B mitered square. Make mitered square.

UPPER LEFT CORNER

With MC, working from left side of upper part of center strip, pick up 23 sts from left edge A block, pick up 1 st in corner, pick up 23 sts along top edge of left side strip, A block. Work mitered square.

With B, pick up 23 sts along left edge of MC block of upper part of center strip, pick up 1 st in corner, pick up 23 sts along top edge of MC mitered square. Work mitered square.

With B, pick up 23 sts along left edge of MC mitered square, pick up 1 st in corner, pick up 23 sts along top edge of left side strip, MC block. Work mitered square.

With MC, pick up 23 sts along left edge of first B mitered square, pick up 1 st in corner, pick up 23 sts along top edge of second B mitered square. Make mitered square.

LOWER RIGHT CORNER

With MC, working from lower part of center strip, pick up 23 sts from right edge of A block, pick up 1 st in corner, pick up 23 sts along bottom edge of right side strip, A block. Work mitered square.

With B, pick up 23 sts along right edge of MC block of lower center strip, pick up 1 st in corner, pick up 23 sts along lower edge of MC mitered square. Work mitered square. With B, pick up 23 sts along right edge of MC mitered square, pick up 1 st in corner, pick up 23 sts along bottom edge of right side strip, MC block. Work mitered square. With MC, pick up 23 sts along right edge of first B mitered square, pick up 1 st in corner, pick up 23 sts along bottom edge of second B mitered square. Make mitered square.

LOWER LEFT CORNER

With MC, working from lower edge of left side strip, pick up 23 sts from bottom edge A block, pick up 1 st in corner, pick up 23 sts along left edge of lower center strip, A block. Work mitered square.

With B, pick up 23 sts along lower edge of MC block of left side strip, pick up 1 st in corner, pick up 23 sts along left edge of MC mitered square. Work mitered square.

With B, pick up 23 sts along bottom edge of MC mitered square, pick up 1 st in corner, pick up 23 sts along left edge of lower center strip, MC block. Work mitered square.

With MC, pick up 23 sts along lower edge of first B mitered square, pick up 1 st in corner, pick up 23 sts along left edge of second B mitered square. Make mitered square.

BORDER

With circular needle and A, beg at lower left corner, pick up 1 st in corner, pm, pick up 41 sts over the next 2 color blocks, remove waste yarn and knit 23 sts, pick up 41 sts along next 2 blocks, pm, *pick up 1 st in corner, pm, pick up 41, knit across 23 sts of holder, pick up 41, pm; rep from * 2 times more (place different-color marker to mark beg and end of round)—424 stitches.

Rnd 1 Purl.

Rnd 2 (inc) Knit corner stitch, sl marker, KF&B, *knit to 1 stitch before marker, KF&B, sl marker, k1, sl marker, KF&B; rep from * twice more; end k to 1 st before marker, KF&B, sl marker.

Rnd 3 Purl.

Cut A; with MC [work rnd 2; purl 1 rnd] twice.

Cut MC; with B, work rnd 2, purl 1 rnd. Repeat rnd 2.

Finishing

Bind off all sts loosely purlwise, removing markers as you come to them. Block lightly to measurements. ∎

My Fair Baby

A series of stripes is complemented perfectly by an unexpected
Fair Isle band knit in the same colors.

DESIGNED BY BRENDA CASTIEL

Knitted Measurements
Approx 25" x 30.5"/63.5cm x 77.5cm

Materials
■ 2 3½oz/100g balls (each approx 220yd/201m) of Cascade Yarns *220 Superwash* (superwash wool) in #821 daffodil (MC)

■ 1 ball each in #884 skyline blue (A), #891 misty olive (B), #874 ridge rock (C), and #817 aran (D)

■ Size 7 (4.5mm) circular needle, 32"/81cm long, *or size to obtain gauge*

Notes
1) Blanket is worked back and forth in rows. Circular needle is used to accommodate large number of sts—do not join.
2) When changing colors, twist yarns on WS to prevent holes in work.

Stripe Pattern A
Work in St st as follows: 2 rows C, 2 rows MC, 2 rows D, 2 rows B, 2 rows A, 2 rows C, 2 rows D, 2 rows MC, 2 rows B, 2 rows C, 2 rows MC, 2 rows A, 2 rows D, 2 rows B.

Stripe Pattern B
Work in St st as follows: 4 rows C, 6 rows MC, 8 rows A, 4 rows B, 6 rows D, 8 rows C, 4 rows A.

Blanket
With MC, cast on 123 sts.
Row 1 (RS) Sl 1 purlwise wyif, knit to end of row. Rep row 1 16 times more, end with a RS row.
Next row (WS) Sl 1 purlwise wyif, k8, purl to last 9 sts, k9.

Next row (RS) Sl 1 purlwise wyif, knit to end of row.
Repeat last 2 rows 7 times more, then first row once, end with a WS row.

BEG CHART PAT
Next row (RS) With MC, sl 1 purlwise wyif, k8, beg chart on row 1, work 8-st rep 13 times, work last st of chart, with MC k9.
Cont as est to end of chart, working first and last 9 sts in garter st pat with MC. Cont in MC only, as follows:
Next row (RS) Sl 1 purlwise wyif, knit to end of row.
Next row (WS) Sl 1 purlwise wyif, k8, purl to last 9 sts, k9.
Rep last 2 rows 11 times, end with a WS row.
Keeping first and last 9 sts in garter st pat with MC, work 28 rows in stripe sequence A, end with a WS row. Cont in MC only, as follows:
Next row (RS) Sl 1 purlwise wyif, knit to end of row.
Next row (WS) Sl 1 purlwise wyif, k8, purl to last 9 sts, k9.

Gauge
20 sts and 28 rows to 4"/10cm over St st using size 7 (4.5mm) needles.
Take time to check gauge.

My Fair Baby

Rep last 2 rows 10 times more, end with a WS row.

Keeping first and last 9 sts in garter st pat with MC, work 40 rows in stripe sequence B, end with a WS row. Cont in MC only, as follows:

Next row (RS) Sl 1 purlwise wyif, knit to end of row.

Next row (WS) Sl 1 purlwise wyif, k8, purl to last 9 sts, k9.

Rep last 2 rows 8 times more, end with a WS row.

TOP EDGING

Row 1 (RS) Sl 1 purlwise wyif, knit to end of row.

Rep last row 16 times more, end with a RS row. Bind off all sts knitwise.

Finishing

Weave in ends. Block to finished measurements. ∎

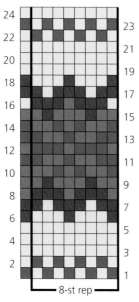

Stitch Key

- MC
- A
- B
- C

Night Houses

Doors of many colors emerge from the landscape of an enchanted mountain village at night—just right for sleepytime.

DESIGNED BY CHRISTINA BEHNKE

Knitted Measurements
Approx 35"/90cm square

Materials
■ 4 3½oz/100g balls (each approx 220yd/201m) Cascade Yarns *220 Superwash* in #1946 silver grey (A)

■ 3 balls in #900 charcoal (B)

■ 1 ball each in #1973 seafoam heather (C), #821 daffodil (D), #808 sunset orange (E), #825 orange (F), #849 dark aqua (G), #827 coral (H)

■ 1 pair size 7 (4.5mm) needles, *or size to obtain gauge*

■ Stitch markers

■ Tapestry needle

Notes
1) Blanket is worked in strips, then seamed.
2) When changing colors in intarsia pattern, twist yarns together to prevent gaps.

Seed Stitch
Row 1 (RS) *K1, p1; rep from * to end of row.
Row 2 (WS) *P1, k1; rep from * to end of row.
Repeat rows 1 and 2 for seed st.

Double Seed Stitch
Row 1 (RS) K3, *p2, k2; rep from * to last 3 sts; p3.
Row 2 (WS) Rep row 1.
Rows 3 and 4 P3, *k2, p2; rep from * to last 3 sts; k3.
Rep rows 1–4 for double seed st.

House Peak Pattern
Instructions are written for light gray house (dark gray house in parentheses).
Row 1 (RS) With A (B), k2; with B (A), k28; with A (B), k2.
Row 2 (WS) With A (B), p3; with B (A), p26; with A (B), p3.
Row 3 With A (B), k4; with B (A), k24; with A (B), k4.
Row 4 With A (B), p5; with B (A), p22; with A (B), p5.
Row 5 With A (B), k6; with B (A), k20; with A (B), k6.
Row 6 With A (B), p7; with B (A), p18; with A (B), p7.
Row 7 With A (B), k8; with B (A), k16; with A (B), k8.
Row 8 With A (B), p9; with B (A), p14; with A (B), p9.
Row 9 With A (B), k10; with B (A), k12; with A (B), k10.
Row 10 With A (B), p11; with B (A), p10; with A (B), p11.
Row 11 With A (B), k12; with B (A), k8; with A (B), k12.
Row 12 With A (B), p13; with B (A), p6; with A (B), p13.
Row 13 With A (B), k14; with B (A), k4; with A (B), k14.
Row 14 With A (B), p15; with B (A), p2; with A (B), p15.

Gauges
20 sts and 30 rows to 4"/10cm over St st using size 7 needles.
20 sts and 34 rows to 4"/10cm over seed st using size 7 needles. *Take time to check gauges.*

Row 15 With A (B), knit.
Row 16 With A (B), purl.

Blanket
STRIP 1
With A, cast on 32 sts. Work in seed st until piece measures 6".
With B, k 1 row, pm in last worked st for beg of house block. Cont in St st until piece measures 9½". Work house peak pat for dark gray house.
With A, work in seed st until piece measures 18".
With B, work in St st until piece measures 24".
With A, k 1 row, pm in last worked st for beg of house block. Cont in St st until piece measures 27½". Work house peak pat for light gray house.
With B, work in double seed st until piece measures 36", ending with a row 4. Bind off on RS.

STRIP 2
With A, cast on 32 sts. Work in St st until piece measures 3". Work in seed st until piece measures 9".
With B, k 1 row, pm in last worked st for beg of house block. Cont in St st until piece measures 12½". Work house peak pat for dark gray house.
With A, work in seed st until piece measures 21". Knit 1 row, pm in last worked st for beg of house block. Cont in St st until piece measures 24½". Work house peak pat for light gray house.
With B, work in double seed st until piece measures 33". Work in St st until piece measures 36". Bind off on RS.

STRIP 3
With B, cast on 32 sts. Purl 1 row, pm in first st of last worked row for beg of house block. Cont in St st until piece measures 3½". Work house peak pat for dark gray house.
With A, work in seed st until piece measures 12". Work in St st until piece measures 18". Work in seed st until piece measures 24". K 1 row, pm in last worked st for beg of house block. Cont in St st until piece measures 27½". Work house peak pat for light gray house.
With B, work in double seed st until piece measures 36", ending with a row 4. Bind off on RS.

STRIP 4
With A, cast on 32 sts. Work in St st until piece measures 3". Work in seed st until piece measures 9".
With B, k 1 row, pm in last worked st for beg of house block. Cont in St st until piece measures 12½". Work house peak pat for dark gray house.
With A, k 1 row, pm in last worked st for beg of house block. Cont in St st until piece measures 18½". Work house peak pat for light gray house.
With B, work in double seed st until piece measures 27". Work in St st until piece measures 33". Work in double seed st until piece measures 36", ending with a row 4. Bind off on RS.

STRIP 5
With A, cast on 32 sts. Work in seed st until piece measures 6".
With B, k 1 row, pm in last worked st for beg of house block. Cont in St st until piece measures 9½". Work house peak pat for dark gray house.
With A, work in seed st until piece measures 18".
With B, work in St st until piece measures 24". Work in double seed st until piece measures 30". With A, k 1 row, pm in last worked st for beg of house block. Cont in St st until piece measures 33½". Work house peak pat for light gray house. Bind off on RS.

STRIP 6
With A, cast on 32 sts. Work in seed st until piece measures 3". Work in St st until piece measures 9". Work in seed st until piece measures 18".
With B, k 1 row, pm in last worked st for beg of house block. Cont in St st until piece measures 21½". Work house peak pat for dark gray house.
With B, work in St st until piece measures 27".
With A, k 1 row, pm in last worked st for beg of house block. Cont in St st until piece measures 30½". Work house peak pat for light gray house.
With B, work in double seed st until piece measures 36", ending with a row 4. Bind off in knit.

Night Houses

DOOR FLAP
With C, cast on 15 sts. Work 14 rows in garter st, ending with a WS row. Bind off, leaving a long tail.
Make a total of 2 flaps each in colors C, D, E, F, G, and H.

To attach, line up bind-off edge between 12th and 13th stitch columns of house block. Using long tail, graft bind-off edge to blanket, keeping edge lined up between these two stitch columns.
Place colors as follows:
Strip 1:
Dark gray house: G; light gray house: E.
Strip 2:
Dark gray house: D; light gray house: H.
Strip 3:
Dark gray house: F; light gray house: C.
Strip 4:
Dark gray house: H; light gray house: G.

Strip 5:
Dark gray house: C; light gray house: D.
Strip 6:
Dark gray house: E; light gray house: F.

Arrange so that strips 1–6 are in order from left to right. Using a length of A, seam together.

Border
Row 1 With C, pick up 180 sts along left side edge of blanket.
Row 2 Kf&b, k to 2 sts before end of row, kf&b, k1—182 sts.
Row 3 With D, knit.
Row 4 Kf&b, k to 2 sts before end of row, kf&b, k1—184 sts.
Row 5 With E, knit.
Row 6 Kf&b, k to 2 sts before end of row, kf&b, k1—186 sts.
Row 7 With F, knit.
Row 8 Kf&b, k to 2 sts before end of row, kf&b, k1—188 sts.
Row 9 With G, knit.
Row 10 Kf&b, k to 2 sts before end of row, kf&b, k1—190 sts.
Rows 11 and 12 With H, knit.
Bind off on RS, leaving a long tail.

Repeat on rem 3 edges of blanket. Using long tail from each bind-off row, graft each corner tog.

Finishing
Weave in ends. Block lightly to measurements. ∎

Monkeying Around

Your little monkey will feel like swinging from the trees wrapped in this banana-yellow blanket.

DESIGNED BY SANDI PROSSER

Knitted Measurements
Approx 26" x 32"/66cm x 81cm

Materials
■ 3 3½oz/100g hanks (each approx 128yd/117m) of Cascade Yarns *128 Superwash* (superwash merino) in #1984 lemon drop (A)

■ 1 hank each in colors #858 ginger (B), #1982 harvest orange (C), #872 bitter chocolate (D), and #817 ecru (E)

■ One each sizes 9 and 10 (5.5mm and 6mm) circular needles, 32" long, *or size to obtain gauge*

■ Crochet hook and waste yarn in contrasting color

Provisional Cast-on
With crochet hook and waste yarn, crochet a chain several stitches longer than the required number of sts to be cast on. Fasten off. With knitting needle, pick up and k the required number of sts in the bumps of the chain, leaving a few empty chains at either end. When directed, "unzip" the sts by undoing the end of the chain and pulling it out, placing the live sts on the needle.

Blanket
With size 10 (6mm) needle and A, cast on 84 sts using provisional cast-on. Starting with a RS row, work in St st until piece measures 5½"/14cm from beg, ending with a WS row.
Next row (RS) K23, work row 1 of chart over next 37 sts, k to end of row.
Next row P24, work row 2 of chart over next 37 sts, p to end of row.
Cont as established, working appropriate row of chart, to end of chart.
Cont even with A, working in St st, until piece measures 29"/73.5cm from beg, end with a WS row.
Change to smaller needle.

UPPER EDGING
Rows 1 and 5 (RS) With D, knit.
Rows 2 and 6 With D, k2, M1, knit to last 2 sts, M1, k2—2 sts inc.
Row 3 With E, knit.
Row 4 With E, k2, M1, knit to last 2 sts, M1, k2—2 sts inc.
Row 7 With B, knit.
Row 8 With B, k2, M1, knit to last 2 sts, M1, k2—2 sts inc.

Gauge
14 sts and 20 rows to 4"/10cm over St st using size 10 (6mm) needle.
Take time to check gauge.

Monkeying Around

Row 9 With C, knit.
Row 10 With C, k2, M1, knit to last 2 sts, M1, k2—2 sts inc.
Row 11 With B, knit. Bind off.

LOWER EDGING
Remove provisional cast-on and place sts onto smaller needles.
Work as for upper edging.

SIDE EDGING
With smaller needles, RS facing, and D, pick up and k 110 sts evenly along side edge of blanket. Starting with row 2, work as for upper edging. Repeat for rem side edge.

Finishing
Sew mitered corner edges. Weave in ends. Block lightly to measurements. ■

Color Key
- MC
- A
- B
- C
- D

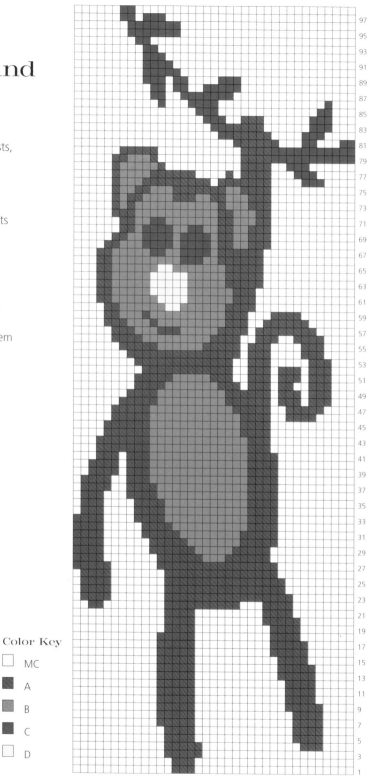

Geometry Class

Soothing pink and green triangles come together to form squares that resemble pretty pinwheels.

DESIGNED BY KAREN GARLINGHOUSE

Knitted Measurements
Approx 22½"/57cm x 30"/76cm

Materials
■ 2 3.5oz/100g balls (each approx 220yd/201m) of Cascade Yarns *220 Superwash* (superwash wool) each in #834 strawberry pink (A) and #831 rose (C)

■ 1 ball each in #850 lime sherbert (B) and #906 chartreuse (D)

■ One pair size 8 (5mm) needles *or size to obtain gauge*

Notes
1) Slip all sts purlwise unless otherwise indicated.
2) Each square measures approx 7½"/19cm on each side.
3) Eight triangles are made, working each triangle from the previous one; then the first and last triangles are sewn together to form a square.

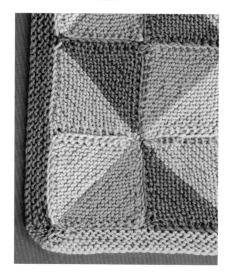

Blanket
SQUARES (MAKE 12)
Triangle 1
With A, cast on 25 sts.
Row 1 (RS) Knit.
Row 2 Sl 1, ssk, knit to last 3 sts, k2tog, k1.
Row 3 Sl 1, knit to end of row.
Rep last 2 rows 10 times—3 sts.
Next row S2KP—1 st. Fasten off.

Triangle 2
With RS facing and B, pick up and k 25 sts along cast-on edge of Triangle 1. Work as given for Triangle 1. Fasten off.

Triangle 3
With RS facing and C, pick up and k 12 sts along right edge of Triangle 2, cast on 1 st, turn—13 sts.
Row 1 (WS) Kfb, k1 tbl, turn.
Row 2 Knit.
Row 3 Sl 1, kfb, k1, k1 tbl, turn.
Row 4 Knit.
Cont as established until all picked-up sts have been worked, end with a WS row—25 sts on needle. Break C and join D.

Triangle 4
Row 1 K25.
Row 2 Sl 1, ssk, knit to last 3 sts, k2tog, k1.
Row 3 Sl 1, knit to end of row.
Rep last 2 rows 10 times—3 sts.
Next row S2KP—1 st. Fasten off.

Triangle 5
Using A, work as given for Triangle 3.

Gauge
20 sts and 40 rows to 4"/10cm over garter st using size 8 (5mm) needles.
Take time to check gauge.

Geometry Class

Triangle 6
Using B, work as given for Triangle 4.

Triangle 7
Using C, work as given for Triangle 3.

Triangle 8
Using D, work as given for Triangle 4. Sew seam between triangles 8 and 1 to form a square.

ASSEMBLY
Sew squares together into 4 rows of 3 squares each, arranging strips so that triangles 1 and 2 are at the top left corner.

Top border
With A, pick up and k 76 sts evenly along top edge of blanket.
Row 1 (WS) Sl 1, kfb, k to last 2 sts, kfb, k1.
Rep row 1 five times, end with a RS row. Bind off all sts knitwise.

Bottom border
With C, pick up and k 76 sts evenly along bottom edge of blanket.
Row 1 (WS) Sl 1, kfb, k to last 2 sts, kfb, k1.
Rep row 1 five times, end with a RS row. Bind off all sts knitwise.

Right side border
With B, pick up and k 94 sts evenly along right side edge of blanket.
Row 1 (WS) Sl 1, kfb, k to last 2 sts, kfb, k1.
Rep row 1 five times, end with a RS row. Bind off all sts knitwise.

Left side border
With B, pick up and k 94 sts evenly along left side edge of blanket.
Row 1 (WS) Sl 1, kfb, k to last 2 sts, kfb, k1.
Rep row 1 five times, end with a RS row. Bind off all sts knitwise.
Sew corners of borders together to form a mitered corner.

Finishing
Weave in all ends. Block lightly to measurements. ∎

Gorgeous Gingham

Red and white gingham checks, knitted big and bold, strike a balance between traditional and modern.

DESIGNED BY LOREN CHERENSKY

Knitted Measurements
Approx 29" x 26"/73.5cm x 66cm

Materials
■ 3 3.5oz/100g hanks (each approx 128yd/117m) Cascade Yarns *128 Superwash* (superwash merino) in #809 really red (MC)

■ 2 hanks in #817 ecru (CC)

■ Size 10 (6mm) circular needle, 32"/80cm long, *or size to obtain gauge*

■ Size H/8 (5mm) crochet hook

Notes
1) Blanket is worked back and forth in rows. Circular needle is used to accommodate large number of sts—do not join.
2) When changing colors, twist yarns on WS to prevent holes and carry yarn not in use loosely across back of work.
3) Do not carry yarn across gingham blocks.

Blanket
With size 10 (6mm) circular needle and MC, cast on 105 sts.

BEG CHART
Row 1 (RS) Work 30-st rep 3 times, then work sts 31–45.
Continue as established, working rows 1–32 of chart pat 3 times, then rows 1–16 once, end with a WS row. Bind off all sts.

Finishing
Block lightly.

EDGING
With crochet hook, right side facing, and CC, work 1 rnd single crochet around outer edge of blanket, working 2 sc into each corner. Join with a slip st to first sc. Fasten off. ■

Gauge
18 sts and 16 rows to 4"/10cm over gingham block pat using size 10 (6mm) circular needle.
Take time to check gauge.

Gorgeous Gingham

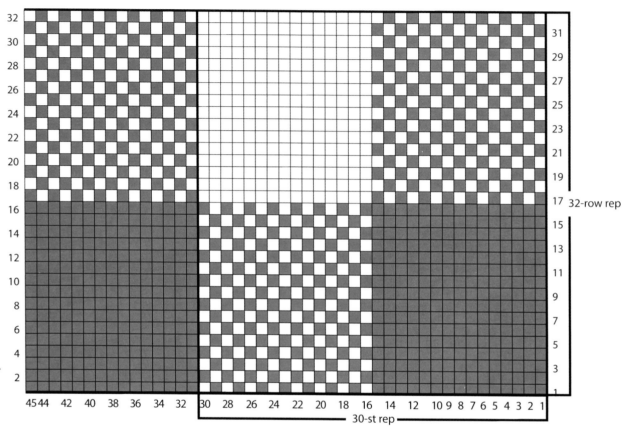

Stitch Key

■ MC, k on RS, p on WS

☐ A, k on RS, p on WS

Quick Tip
Wind small amounts of yarn onto bobbins
to work each gingham block.

Baby Makes Three

Three bold stripes and a beguiling texture complement one another perfectly in this striking afghan.

DESIGNED BY LINDA MEDINA

Knitted Measurements
Approx 25" x 46"/63.5cm x 117cm

Materials
■ 3 3½oz/100g hanks (each approx 128yd/117m) Cascade Yarns *128 Superwash* (superwash merino) each in #905 celery (A), #1960 pacific (B), and #1910 summer sky heather (C)

■ Size 7 (4.5mm) circular needle, 32"/80cm long, *or size to obtain gauge*

■ Stitch markers

Note
Circular needle is used to accommodate large number of sts—do not join.

Pattern Stitch
(over a multiple of 12 sts plus 7)
Row 1 (RS) K2, *p3, k3, yo, S2KP, yo, k3; rep from * to last 5 sts, p3, k2.
Row 2 and all WS rows K the knit sts, p the purl sts and yarn overs.
Row 3 K2, *p3, k1, k2tog, yo, k3, yo, SKP, k1; rep from * to last 5 sts, p3, k2.
Row 5 Rep row 1.
Row 7 Knit.
Row 9 K2, *yo, S2KP, yo, k3, p3, k3; rep from * to last 5 sts, yo, S2KP, yo, k2.

Row 11 *K2tog, yo, k3, yo, SKP, k1, p3, k1; rep from * to last 7 sts, k2tog, yo, k3, yo, SKP.
Row 13 Rep row 9.
Row 15 Knit.
Row 16 Rep row 2.
Rep rows 1–16 for pat st.

Blanket
With A, cast on 123 sts. K 5 rows.
**Next row (RS) K4, place marker (pm), work row 1 of pat st to last 4 sts, pm, k4.
Next row (WS) K4, sl marker, work row 2 of pat st to last 4 sts, sl marker, k4.
Cont to work pat st in this way, working border sts outside markers in garter st (k every row), until the 16-row rep of pat st has been worked 5 times, then work rows 1–14 once more.** Cut A and join B.
With B, work rows 15 and 16 of pat st, then rep between **'s. Cut B and join C.
With C, work rows 15 and 16 of pat st, then work 16-row rep of pat st 6 times, keeping border sts in garter st. K 5 rows. Bind off.

Finishing
Weave in all ends. Block lightly to measurements. ■

Gauge
19 sts and 26 rows to 4"/10cm over pat stitch using size 7 circular (4.5mm) needle.
Take time to check gauge.

In the Navy

Freshen up classic navy blue by striping it with bright baby colors.

DESIGNED BY MARY BETH TEMPLE

Knitted Measurements
Approx 36" x 34"/91.5cm x 86.5cm

Materials
■ 4 3½oz/100g hanks (each approx 220yd/201m) Cascade Yarns *220 Superwash* (superwash wool) in #813 blue velvet (MC)

■ 1 skein each in #824 yellow (A), #887 wasabi (B), #820 lemon (C), and #1940 peach (D)

■ Size 7 (4.5mm) circular needle, 32"/80cm long, *or size to obtain gauge*

Notes
1) Use separate balls of each color for each block.
2) Wind MC onto bobbins for vertical panels—do not carry across back of work.
3) When changing colors, twist yarns on WS to prevent holes.

Blankets
With MC, cast on 155 sts. Work 13 rows in garter st (k every row), end with a RS row.
Set-up row (WS) With MC, k10, p30, [k5, p30] 3 times, k10.

BEG BLOCK PAT 1
Row 1 (RS) With MC, k10; with A, k30; with MC, k5; with B, k30; with MC, k5; with C, k30; with MC, k5; with D, k30; with MC, k10.
Row 2 With MC, k10; with D, p30; with MC, k5; with C, p30; with MC, k5; with B, p30; with MC, k5; with A, p30; with MC, k10.
Row 3 With MC, knit.
Row 4 With MC, k10, p30, [k5, p30] 3 times, k10.
Rep last 4 rows 13 times more, then rows 1 to 3 once more, end with a RS row.
With MC, work 5 rows in garter st, end with a WS row.

BEG BLOCK PAT 2
Row 1 (RS) With MC, k10; with D, k30; with MC, k5; with C, k30; with MC, k5; with A, k30; with MC, k5; with B, k30; with MC, k10.
Row 2 With MC, k10; with B, p30; with MC, k5; with A, p30; with MC, k5; with C, p30; with MC, k5; with D, p30; with MC, k10.
Row 3 With MC, knit.
Row 4 With MC, k10, p30, [k5, p30] 3 times, k10.
Rep last 4 rows 13 times more, then rows 1 to 3 once more, end with a RS row.
With MC, work 5 rows in garter st, end with a WS row.

BEG BLOCK PAT 3
Row 1 (RS) With MC, k10; with A, k30; with MC, k5; with B, k30; with MC, k5; with D, k30; with MC, k5; with C, k30; with MC, k10.
Row 2 With MC, k10; with C, p30; with MC, k5; with D, p30; with MC, k5; with B, p30; with MC, k5; with A, p30; with MC, k10.
Row 3 With MC, knit.
Row 4 With MC, k10, p30, [k5, p30] 3 times, k10.
Rep last 4 rows 13 times more, then rows 1 to 3 once more, end with a RS row.
With MC, work 13 rows in garter st, end with a WS row. Bind off all sts knitwise.

Finishing
Weave in ends. Block to finished measurements. ■

Gauge
19 sts and 26 rows to 4"/10cm over St st using size 7 (4.5mm) circular needle.
Take time to check gauge.

Sweet Safari

It's hard to resist this charming spotted giraffe enjoying a leisurely snack while basking in the sun.

DESIGNED BY EMILY RUBIN

■■■■▶

Knitted Measurements
Approx 35"/90cm square

Materials
■ 5 3½oz/100g balls (each approx 220yd/201m) Cascade Yarns *220 Superwash* (superwash wool) in #1942 mint (MC)

■ 1 ball each in #1976 sunshine heather (A), #819 chocolate (B), #823 burnt orange (C), and #906 chartreuse (D)

■ One size 7 (4.5mm) circular needle, 32"/80cm long, *or size to obtain gauge*

Notes
1) Charts are worked in St st throughout.

2) Blanket is worked back and forth in rows. Circular needle is used to accommodate large number of sts—do not join.

Seed Stitch
(over an odd number of stitches)
Row 1 (RS) *K1, p1; rep from *, end k1. Rep row 1 for seed st.

Blanket
With MC, cast on 185 sts. Work 12 rows in seed st, end with a WS row.
Next row (RS) Work first 9 sts in seed st, k to last 9 sts, work in seed st to end of row.
Next row Work first 9 sts in seed st, p to last 9 sts, work in seed st to end of row. Cont as now established, working first and last 9 sts in seed st, until piece measures 8"/20.5cm from beg, end with a WS row.

BEG CHART A
Next row (RS) Work 45 sts in pat as established, work row 1 of Chart A over next 95 sts, work in pat to end of row.
Next row Work 45 sts in pat, work row 2 of Chart A over next 95 sts, work in pat to end of row.
Cont as established, working appropriate row of chart, to end of chart (row 108).
Next row (RS) Work first 9 sts in seed st, k to last 9 sts, work in seed st to end of row.
Next row Work first 9 sts in seed st, p to last 9 sts, work in seed st to end of row.

BEG CHART B
Next row (RS) Work 96 sts in pat, work row 1 of Chart B over next 33 sts, work in pat to end of row.
Next row Work 56 sts in pat, work row 2 of Chart B over next 33 sts, work in pat to end of row.
Cont as now established, working appropriate row of chart, to end of chart (row 40).
Next row (RS) Work first 9 sts in seed st, k to last 9 sts, work in seed st to end of row.
Next row Work first 9 sts in seed st, p to last 9 sts, work in seed st to end of row. Rep last 2 rows until piece measures 33½"/85cm from beg, end with a WS row.
Work 12 rows in seed st, end with a WS row. Bind off all sts in pat.

Finishing
Weave in ends. Block lightly to finished measurements. ■

Gauge
21 sts and 27 rows to 4"/10cm over St st using size 7 (4.5mm) needle.
Take time to check gauge.

Sweet Safari

CHART B

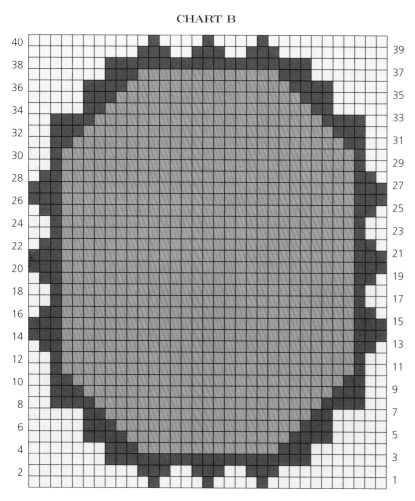

Color Key

☐ Mint (MC)

▨ Sunshine Heather (A)

▨ Chocolate (B)

▨ Burnt Orange (C)

▨ Chartreuse (D)

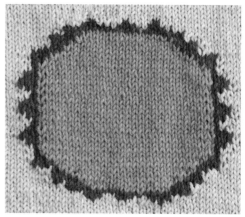

Sunny Bunnies

Little animal lovers will love to snuggle up with these precious yellow bunnies crafted from cables and bobbles.

DESIGNED BY LINDA CYR

Knitted Measurements
40"/101.5cm square

Materials
- 8 3.5 oz/100g skeins (each approx 128yd/117m) of Cascade *128 Superwash* (merino wool) in #1984 lemon drop
- Size 9 (5.5mm) circular needle, 32" long, *or size to obtain gauge*
- Cable needle
- Size I/9 (5.5mm) crochet hook

Moss Stitch
(over a multiple of 2 sts)
Rows 1 and 2 (K1, p1) across.
Rows 3 and 4 (P1, k1) across.
Repeat rows 1–4 for moss st.

Bobble
Row 1 (K1, p1, k1, p1, k1) in one st, turn.
Rows 2–4 K5, turn.
Row 5 Sl 3, k2tog, pass 3 slipped sts over the k2tog.

Bunny Block
Row 1 (WS) K3, p3, m1, p3, k3.
Row 2 Sl 3 to cn, hold in back, k3, k3 from cn, make bobble in next st, sl 3 to cn, hold in front, sl rem st from bobble to LH needle, k2tog, k2, k3 from cn.
Rows 3, 5, 7, and 9 Purl.
Rows 4, 6, and 8 Knit.
Row 10 Sl 3 to cn, hold in front, p1, k3 from cn, k4, sl 1 to cn, hold in back, k3, p1 from cn.
Row 11 K1, p10, k1.
Row 12 P1, sl 3 to cn, hold in front, p1, k3 from cn, k2, sl 1 to cn, hold in back, k3, p1 from cn, p1.
Rows 13, 15, and 17 K2, p8, k2.
Row 14 P2, sl 2 to cn, hold in back, k2, k2 from cn, sl 2 to cn, hold in front, k2, k2 from cn, p2.
Row 16 P2, k8, p2
Row 18 P2, sl 2 to cn, hold in front, k2, k2 from cn, sl 2 to cn, hold in back, k2, k2 from cn, p2.
Row 19 K2, p8, k2.
Row 20 P2, sl 1 to cn, hold in back, k3, p1 from cn, sl 3 to cn, hold in front, p1, k3 from cn, p2.
Row 21 K2, p3, k2, p3, k2.
Row 22 P2, k1, k2tog, m1 purlwise, p2, m1 purlwise, ssk, k1, p2.
Row 23 K2, p2, k4, p2, k2.
Row 24 P2, k2tog, m1 purlwise, p4, m1 purlwise, ssk, p2.

Blanket
Cast on 148 sts.
Rows 1–19 Sl 1 purlwise wyib, work moss st over 146 sts, end k1.
Rows 20–35 Sl 1 purlwise wyib, work moss st over 12 sts, work rev St st (purl on RS, knit on WS) over 122 sts, work in moss st over 12 sts, k1.
Rows 36–59 Sl 1 purlwise wyib, moss st over 12 sts, work rev St st over 15 sts, [work bunny block over 12 sts, rev St st over 28 sts] twice, work bunny block over 12 sts, work rev St st over 15 sts, work moss st over 12 sts, k1.
Rows 60–95 Repeat row 20.
Rows 96–119 Sl 1 purlwise wyib, work moss st over 12 sts, work rev St st over 35 sts, work bunny block over 12 sts, work rev St st over 28 sts, work bunny block over 12 sts, work rev St st over 35 sts, work moss st over 12 sts, k1.

Gauge
15 sts and 21 rows to 4"/10cm over reverse St st using size 9 (5.5mm) circular needle.
Take time to check gauge.

Sunny Bunnies

Rows 120–155 Repeat row 20.
Rows 156–179 Repeat rows 36–59.
Rows 180–195 Repeat row 20.
Rows 196–213 Repeat row 1.
Row 214 Bind off in pat, leave last lp on needle, do not cut yarn.

Finishing

Place crochet hook into last lp. With RS of blanket facing, work a rnd of sl st around edge of blanket—1 st per st along top and bottom edges, 1 st per row along sides. Sl to beg and fasten off. Weave in ends and steam block. ∎

15

Zig and Zag

A playful combination of colors and pointy zigzag edges add flair to a simple chevron pattern.

DESIGNED BY HOLLI YEOH

Knitted Measurements
Approx 24" x 33"/61cm x 84cm

Materials
■ 1 3½oz/100g ball (each approx 220yd/201m) Cascade Yarns *220 Superwash* (superwash wool) each in #859 lake chelan heather (A), #1949 lavender (B), #1910 summer sky heather (C), #1947 amethyst heather (D), #1919 turtle (E), #1970 montmartre (F), #905 celery (G) and #1948 mystic purple (H)

■ One pair size 8 (5mm) needles, *or size to obtain gauge*

Notes
1) Slip all sts purlwise unless otherwise indicated.
2) This blanket uses a modular technique called strip knitting. The blanket is constructed out of narrow strips, which are joined together as they are knit.
3) When joining strips, pick up the selvage st through both lps.

Stitch Glossary
k2tog bind-off *K2tog, place resulting st back on LH needle; rep from * until all sts have been worked. Fasten off.
kf&b Inc 1 by knitting into the front and back of next st.

Left-Leaning Modular Strip Pattern
Row 1 (RS) K1, k2tog, k to last 2 sts, kf&b, yfwd, sl 1. With right-hand needle, insert tip through next selvage loop on previous strip as if to purl, wrap yarn around needle purlwise and pull loop back through selvage loop, thus picking up and purling a new st. Psso.
Row 2 (WS) Sl 1 kwise, k to last st, yfwd, sl 1.
Repeat these 2 rows to desired length for left-leaning modular strip pat.

Right-Leaning Modular Strip Pattern
Row 1 (RS) Kf&b, k to last 3 sts, k2tog, yfwd, sl 1. With right-hand needle, insert tip through next selvage lp on previous strip as if to purl, wrap yarn around needle pwise and pull lp back through selvage lp, thus picking up and purling a new st. Psso.
Row 2 (WS) Sl 1 knitwise, k to last st, yfwd, sl 1.
Repeat these 2 rows to desired length for right-leaning modular strip pat.

Blanket
STRIP 1
With A, cast on 14 sts.
Row 1 (RS) Kf&b, k to last 3 sts, k2tog, yfwd, sl 1.
Row 2 K to last st, yfwd, sl 1.
Rep last 2 rows 5 times more, end with a WS row. Break A.
Using assembly diagram as a guide, work 14 rows as established for each color in sequence until 16 blocks have been worked, end with a WS row. Bind off using k2tog bind-off.

Gauge
18 sts and 35 rows to 4"/10cm over garter st using size 8 (5mm) needles. *Take time to check gauge.*

Zig and Zag

STRIP 2

With RS of previous strip facing and E, pick up and k 1 st in lower-most cast-on st below first selvage lp on right-hand edge. Cast on an additional 13 sts—14 sts.

Work left-leaning modular strip pat for 12 rows, end with a WS row.

Using assembly diagram as a guide, work 14 rows as established for each color in sequence until 16 blocks have been worked, end with a WS row. Bind off using k2tog bind-off.

STRIP 3

With RS of previous strip facing and G, pick up and k 1 st in lower-most cast-on st below first selvage lp on right-hand edge. Cast on an additional 13 sts—14 sts.

Work right-leaning modular strip pat for 12 rows, end with a WS row.

Using assembly diagram as a guide, work 14 rows as established for each color in sequence until 16 blocks have been worked, end with a WS row. Bind off using k2tog bind-off.

STRIPS 4, 6, 8, 10, AND 12

Work as given for Strip 2, using appropriate color following assembly diagram.

STRIPS 5, 7, 9, AND 11

Work as given for Strip 3, using appropriate color following assembly diagram.

Finishing

Weave in all ends. Block lightly to measurements. ∎

Color Key

- 859 Lake Chelan Heather (A)
- 1949 Lavender (B)
- 1910 Summer Sky Heather (C)
- 1947 Amethyst Heather (D)
- 1919 Turtle (E)
- 1970 Montmartre (F)
- 905 Celery (G)
- 1948 Mystic Purple (H)

16

Lavender Lace

Squares of Swedish lace are bordered in moss stitch for a beautiful blend of complementary textures.

DESIGNED BY KAREN KENDRICK-HANDS

Knitted Measurements
43" x 43"/109cm x 109cm

Materials
■ 6 3½oz/100g balls (each approx 220yd/201m) of Cascade Yarns *220 Superwash* (superwash wool) in #842 iris

■ Size 8 (5mm) circular needle, 32"/80cm long, *or size to obtain gauge*

■ 3 additional size 8 (5mm) circular needles, 32"/80cm long, for edging (optional)

■ Size G/6 (4mm) crochet hook

■ 10 stitch markers (optional)

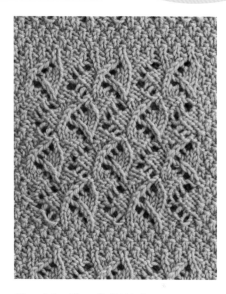

Double Seed Stitch
(over an odd number of sts)
Row 1 [RS] Sl 1 wyib, *k1, p1; rep from *to end.
Row 2 Sl 1 wyib, k the knit sts and p the purl sts.
Row 3 Sl 1 wyif p the knit sts and k the purl sts.
Row 4 Sl 1wyif, k the knit sts and p the purl sts.
Rep rows 1–4 for double seed st.
Pattern blocks [reps] are in brackets.

Crochet Cast-on
1. Place a slip knot on the crochet hook. Holding knitting needle and yarn in LH with needle under the hook, wrap yarn around hook from back to front. Draw lp through slip knot.
2. Bring the yarn to the back under the needle, wrap the yarn as before and draw through the lp on the hook. Rep this step until one less than the desired number of sts has been cast on.
3. Place rem lp from hook on needle.

Notes
1) Blanket is worked in one piece in rows. Circular needle is used to maintain large number of sts—do not join.
2) Placing stitch markers to separate the blocks of lace from the double seed stitch will make it easier to keep the patterns aligned. Sl markers every row.

Blanket
With crochet hook and circular needle, cast on 169 sts.
Work 8 rows in double seed st.
BEG CHART
*Next row (RS) Work 8 sts in double seed st as established, [work row 1 of chart, work 7 sts in in double seed st as

Gauges
16 sts and 26 rows to 4"/10cm over double seed st using size 8 (5mm) needle.
Swedish lace block: 25 sts and 36 rows to 5" x 5½"/2.5cm x 14cm. *Take time to check gauges.*

Lavender Lace

Rep from * 5 times more. Bind off. Do not break yarn.

EDGING
Note Edging is worked in the round; more than 1 circular needle may be used to accommodate large number of sts comfortably.
With RS facing and last lp on needle, working through the outside half of each edge st, pick up and k 1 st in each st along entire outside edge of blanket.
Rnd 1 [*(K1, yo, k1, yo, k1) in next st, k1, (p1, yo, p1, yo, p1) in next st, p1, (k1, yo, k1, yo, k1) in next st, k1 (p1, yo, p1, yo, p1) in next st, p2tog; rep from * to corner, **(k1, yo, k1, yo, k1) in next st, ssk, (p1, yo, p1, yo, p1) in next st, p2tog; rep from ** to corner] twice.
Bind off in k6, p6 rib.
Block gently to open lace. ■

established] 4 times, work row 1 of chart, work in double seed st to end.
Cont to work chart in this manner until row 18 is complete. Rep rows 1–18 once more.
Work 8 rows in double seed st.

Stitch Key

☐	K on RS, p on WS
▬	P on RS, k on WS
◿	K2tog on RS, p2tog on WS
◺	Ssk on RS, ssp on WS
◿	P2tog on RS, k2tog on WS
◺	Ssp on RS, ssk on WS
Ⓞ	Yo

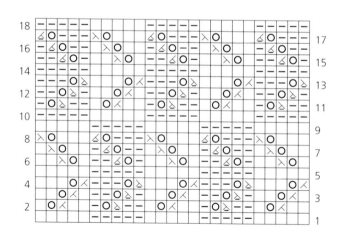

Modern Art

This mod throw starts with soft gray stripes and adds blocks of color for a little pizzazz.

DESIGNED BY HOLLI YEOH

Knitted Measurements
Approx 25" x 34"/63.5cm x 86.5cm

Materials
■ 2 3½oz/100g balls (each approx
220yd/200m) of Cascade Yarns *220
Superwash* (superwash wool) each in
#1946 silver grey (A) and #900
charcoal (B)

■ 1 3½oz/100g ball (each approx
220yd/200m) of Cascade *220 Superwash*
(superwash wool) each in #826 tangerine
(C) and #1975 provence (D)

■ Size 7 (4.5mm) circular needle,
36"/91cm long, *or size to obtain gauge*

■ Size 8 (5mm) circular needle, 36"/91cm
long, *or size to obtain gauge*

■ Bobbins (optional)

Notes
1) When changing colors, bring new
color up from under old to avoid gaps.
2) Wind yarn onto separate bobbins or
small balls for easier handling.
3) Throughout blanket, use smaller
needle for rows that contain color A
and larger needle for rows that contain
color B.

Blanket
With smaller needle and C, using long-
tail method, cast on 16 sts; with A, cast
on 93 sts; with D, cast on 8 sts; with A,
cast on 8 sts—125 sts. Do not join; work
back and forth in rows.
Row 1 (WS) With A, k8; with D, k8; with
A, k to last 16 sts; with C, k16.
Row 2 (RS) With C, k16; with A, k to last
16 sts; with D, k8; with A, k8.
Rows 3–14 Rep rows 1–2 six times more.
Row 15 Rep row 1.
Change to larger needle.
Row 16 With B, k to last 16 sts; with D,
k8, with B, k8.
Row 17 With B, k8; with D, k8; with B,
p to last 8 sts, k8.
Rows 18–25 Rep rows 16–17 four
times more.
Change to smaller needle (continue
changing needles as est throughout).
Row 26 With A, k to last 16 sts; with D,
k8; with A, k8.
Row 27 With A, k8, with D, k8, with A,
k to end.
Rows 28–41 Rep rows 26–27 seven
times more.

Gauges
19 sts and 40 rows to 4"/10cm over garter st using size 7 (4.5mm) needle.
19 sts and 25 rows to 4"/10cm over St st using size 8 (5mm) needle. *Take time to check gauges.*

Modern Art

Row 42 With C, k8; with B, k to last 16 sts; with D, k8; with B, k8.
Row 43 With B, k8; with D, k8, with B, p to last 8 sts; with C, k8.
Rows 44–51 Rep rows 42–43 four times more.
Row 52 With A, k8; with D, k8; with A, k to last 16 sts; with C, k8, with A, k8.
Row 53 With a, k8; with C, k8; with A, k to last 16 sts; with D, k8; with A, k8.
Rows 54–67 Rep rows 52–53 seven times more.
Rows 68–77 Rep rows 42–51.
Row 78 With A, k8; with D, k8; with A, k to last 16 sts; with D, k8; with A, k8.
Rows 79–93 Rep row 78 fifteen times more.
Row 94 With C, k8; with B, k to end.
Row 95 With B, k8, p to last 8 sts; with C, k8.
Rows 96–103 Rep rows 94–95 four times more.
Row 104 With A, k to last 8 sts; with D, k8.
Row 105 With D, k8; with A, k to end.
Rows 106–119 Rep rows 104–105 seven times more.
Row 120 With B, k to last 8 sts; with C, k8.
Row 121 With C, k8; with B, p to last 8 sts, k8.
Rows 122–129 Rep rows 120–121 four times more.
Row 130 With C, k8; with A, k to last 8 sts; with D, k8.
Row 131 With D, k8; with A, k to last 8 sts; with C, k8.
Rows 132–145 Rep rows 130–131 seven times more.
Row 146 With B, knit.

Row 147 With B, k8, p to last 8 sts, k8.
Rows 148–155 Rep rows 146–147 four times more.
Rows 156–171 Rep rows 104–119.
Rows 172–181 Rep rows 146–155.
Row 182 With D, k32; with A, k to end.
Row 183 With A, k93; with D, k32.
Rows 184–197 Rep rows 182–183 seven times more.
Rows 198–207 Rep rows 146–155.
Row 208 With A, k8; with C, k12; with A, k to last 8 sts; with D, k8.
Row 209 With D, k8; with A, k to last 20 sts; with C, k12; with A, k8.
Rows 210–223 Rep rows 208–209 seven times more.
Row 224 With B, k8; with C, k12; with B, k to last 8 sts; with D, k8.
Row 225 With D, k8; with A, p to last 20 sts; with C, k12; with A, k8.
Rows 226–233 Rep rows 224–225 four times more.
Rows 234–249 Rep rows 208–223.
Row 250 With B, k8; with C, k12; with B, k to last 16 sts; with C, k8; with B, k8.
Row 251 With B, k8; with C, k8; with B, p to last 20 sts; with C, k12; with B, k8.
Rows 252–259 Rep rows 250–251 four times more.
Row 260 With A, k8; with C, k12; with A, k to last 16 sts; with C, k8; with A, k8.
Row 261 With A, k8; with C, k8; with A, k to last 20 sts; with C, k12; with A, k8.
Rows 262–275 Rep rows 260–261 seven times more.
Bind off in pat.

Finishing
Weave in ends. Block lightly to measurements. ∎

Modern Art

Color Key

- ☐ Silver Grey (A)
- ■ Charcoal (B)
- ☐ Tangerine (C)
- ■ Provence (D)

Finely Woven

This entrelac beauty features a pretty bobbled border and soothing shades of green and blue.

DESIGNED BY ROSEMARY DRYSDALE

Knitted Measurements
Approx 28" x 30"/71cm x 76cm

Materials
■ 3 3½oz/100g balls (each approx 220yd/200m) of Cascade Yarns *220 Superwash* (superwash wool) each in #897 baby denim (A) and #1942 mint (B)

■ One pair size 6 (4mm) needles *or size to obtain gauge*

■ Size F/5 (3.75mm) crochet hook

Blanket
With A, cast on 96 sts.

BASE TRIANGLES
*Row 1 (WS) P2, turn.
Row 2 (RS) K2, turn.
Row 3 P3, turn.
Row 4 K3, turn.
Row 5 P4, turn.
Row 6 K4, turn.
Row 7 P5, turn.
Row 8 K5, turn.
Row 9 P6, turn.

Row 10 K6, turn.
Row 11 P7, turn.
Row 12 K7, turn.
Row 13 P8, do not turn.
Rep from * for 11 more triangles—12 triangles made. Turn.

RH CORNER TRIANGLE
Join B and work as foll:
Row 1 (RS) K2, turn.
Row 2 (WS) P2, turn.
Row 3 Inc in first st by knitting into front and back of st, ssk, turn.
Row 4 P3, turn.
Row 5 Inc in first st, k1, ssk, turn.
Row 6 P4, turn.
Row 7 Inc in first st, k2, ssk, turn.
Row 8 P5, turn.
Row 9 Inc in first st, k3, ssk, turn.
Row 10 P6, turn.
Row 11 Inc in first st, k4, ssk, turn.
Row 12 P7, turn.
Row 13 Inc in first st, k5, ssk, do not turn.
The RH corner triangle in B is complete. Leave 8 sts on RH needle.

Gauge
24 sts and 34 rows to 4"/10cm over St st using size 6 (4mm) needles.
Take time to check gauge.

Finely Woven

RS RECTANGLES

Cont with B as foll:

*Pick-up row (RS) Pick up and k 8 sts evenly along edge of next triangle/rectangle, turn.

Row 1 (WS) [P1, k1] 4 times, turn.

Row 2 P1, k1, p1, k1, p1, k1, p1, ssk (with last st of rectangle and first st of next triangle/rectangle), turn.

Row 3 [P1, k1] 4 times, turn.

Row 4 K1, p1, k1, p1, k1, p1, k1, ssp, turn.

Rows 5–16 Rep rows 1–4 three times. Do not turn at end of last row.

Rep from * across row—11 RS rectangles have been worked.

LH CORNER TRIANGLE

Cont with B as foll:

Pick-up row (RS) Pick up and k 8 sts along edge of last triangle/rectangle, turn.

Row 1 P2tog, p6, turn.

Row 2 K7, turn.

Row 3 P2tog, p5, turn.

Row 4 K6, turn.

Row 5 P2tog, p4, turn.

Row 6 K5, turn.

Row 7 P2tog, p3, turn.

Row 8 K4, turn.

Row 9 P2tog, p2, turn.

Row 10 K3, turn.

Row 11 P2tog, p1, turn.

Row 12 K2, turn.

Row 13 P2tog, do not turn—1 st remains on RH needle.

WS RECTANGLES

Cont with A as foll:

Pick-up row (WS) Pick up and p 7 sts evenly along edge of triangle just worked—8 sts on RH needle, turn.

*Row 1 K8, turn.

Row 2 P7, p2tog (with last st of rectangle and first st of next triangle/rectangle), turn.

Rows 3–16 Rep rows 1 and 2 seven times. Do not turn.

Next row (WS) Pick up and p 8 sts evenly along edge of next RS rectangle. Turn. Rep from * across row—12 WS rectangles have been worked. Turn.

**Work a RH corner triangle.

Work a row of RS rectangles. Do not turn.

Work a LH corner triangle.

Work a row of WS rectangles.

Rep from ** until there are 13 rows of RS rectangles.

Work one more LH corner triangle—1 st remains on the RH needle. Do not turn.

END TRIANGLES

Cont with A as foll:

*Pick-up row (WS) Pick up and p 7 sts evenly along edge of triangle just worked—8 sts on RH needle. Turn.

Row 1 (RS) K8, turn.

Row 2 P2tog, p5, p2tog, turn.

Row 3 K7, turn.

Row 4 P2tog, p4, p2tog, turn.

Row 5 K6, turn.

Row 6 P2tog, p3, p2tog, turn.

Row 7 K5, turn.

Row 8 P2tog, p2, p2tog, turn.

Row 9 K4, turn.

Row 10 P2tog, p1, p2tog, turn.

Row 11 K3, turn.

Row 12 P2tog, p2tog, turn.

Row 13 K2, turn.

Row 14 P2tog, p2tog, pass 1st st over 2nd st—1 st remains on RH needle. Rep from * across row, picking up sts along edge of rectangle instead of triangle.

Fasten off rem st.

CROCHET EDGING

With RS facing and crochet hook, join A.

Rnd 1 Work sc evenly around entire outside edge of blanket, working 3 sc in each corner, working last 2 lps of last sc with B.

Rnd 2 With B, *(yo and draw up a lp) 3 times in next st, yo and draw through all 7 lps on hook (bobble made), ch 1, skip 1 st; rep from * around, working one bobble in each corner sc without skipping sts.

Rnd 3 With A, work sc in top of each bobble and into each ch-1.

Fasten off.

Finishing

Weave in all ends. Block piece lightly to measurements. ∎

Baby Beluga

A gentle gray giant has a whale of a time swimming in a cool blue background.

DESIGNED BY MARGEAU SOBOTI

Knitted Measurements
Approx 41" x 31"/104cm x 79cm

Materials
■ 7 3½oz/100g hanks (each approx 128yd/117m) Cascade Yarns *128 Superwash* (superwash merino) in #896 blue horizon (MC)

■ 1 hank each in #1946 silver (A) and #813 blue velvet (B)

■ One size 10½ (6.5mm) circular needle, 32"/80cm long, *or size to obtain gauge*

■ Size J/10 (6mm) crochet hook.

Notes
1) Blanket is worked back and forth in rows. Circular needle is used to accommodate large number of sts—do not join.
2) When changing colors, twist yarns on WS to prevent holes. Carry yarn not in use loosely across back of work.
3) Whale motif is worked in St st on a garter st background, following chart.

Blanket
With circular needle and MC, cast on 135 sts. Work 16 rows in garter st (k every row), end with a WS row.

BEG CHART
Next row (RS) K10, work row 1 of Chart A over next 40 sts, k to end of row.
Next row K85, work row 2 of Chart A over next 40 sts, k to end of row.
Cont as established to end of chart (row 36).
Cont in garter st until piece measures 31"/79cm from beg, end with a WS row. Bind off all sts.

Finishing
Block to finished measurements.

EDGING
With crochet hook, right side facing, and A, work 1 rnd single crochet around outer edge of blanket, working 2 sc into each corner. Join with a slip st to first sc. Fasten off.

EMBROIDERY
Using photo as a guide, with B, embroider three rows of chain stitches as water coming from the whale's blowhole. With B, embroider a row of chain stitches for the eye and 3 running sts as eyelashes. ■

Gauge
15 sts and 28 rows to 4"/10cm over garter st using size 10½ (6.5mm) needles.
Take time to check gauge.

Baby Beluga

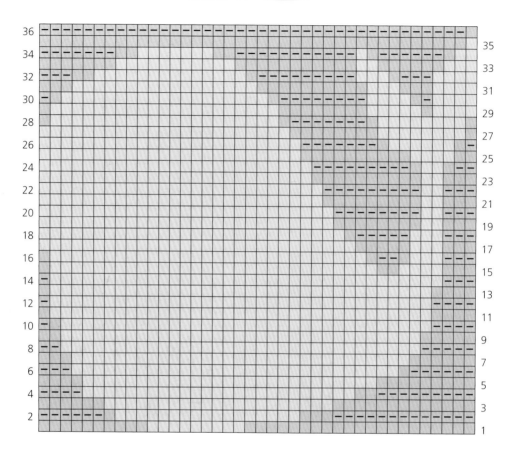

Stitch & Color Key

☐ MC, k on RS, p on WS

⊟ MC, k on RS, k on WS

☐ A, k on RS, p on WS

Ruby Red

Simple garter and stockinette squares are broken up with eyelets to form a gem of a geometric pattern.

DESIGNED BY VERONICA PARSONS

Finished Measurements
Approx 32" x 32"/81cm x 81cm

Materials
■ 6 3½oz/100g (each approx 128yd/117m) hanks of Cascade Yarns *128 Superwash* (superwash merino) in #809 really red

■ Size 10 (6mm) circular needle, 24"/60cm long, *or size to obtain gauge*

■ Stitch markers

Moss Stitch
(over an odd number of sts)
Row 1 (WS) K1, *p1, k1; rep from * to end.
Rows 2 and 3 P1, *k1, p1; rep from * to end.
Row 4 K1, *p1, k1; rep from * to end.
Rep rows 1–4 for moss st.

Geometric Pattern
(over multiple of 14 sts plus 1)
Row 1 (RS) P1, *k6, k2tog, k5, yo, p1; rep from * to end.
Rows 2, 4, 6, 8, 10, and 12 *K1, p7, k6; rep from * to last st, k1.

Row 3 P1, *k6, k2tog, k4, yo, k1, p1; rep from * to end.
Row 5 P1, *k6, k2tog, k3, yo, k2, p1; rep from * to end.
Row 7 P1, *k6, k2tog, k2, yo, k3, p1; rep from * to end.
Row 9 P1, *k6, k2tog, k1, yo, k4, p1; rep from * to end.
Row 11 P1, *k6, k2tog, yo, k5, p1; rep from * to end.
Row 13 P1, *yo, k5, ssk, k6, p1; rep from * to end.
Rows 14, 16, 18, 20, and 22 *K7, p7; rep from * to last st, k1.
Row 15 P1, *k1, yo, k4, ssk, k6, p1; rep from * to end.
Row 17 P1, *k2, yo, k3, ssk, k6, p1; rep from * to end.
Row 19 P1, *k3, yo, k2, ssk, k6, p1; rep from * to end.
Row 21 P1, *k4, yo, k1, ssk, k6, p1; rep from * to end.
Row 23 P1, *k5, yo, ssk, k6, p1; rep from * to end.
Row 24 *K7, p7; rep from * to last st, k1.
Rep rows 1–24 for geometric pat.

Note
Circular needle is used to accommodate large number of sts—do not join.

Gauge
14 sts and 24 rows to 4"/10cm over pattern st using size 10 (6mm) needle.
Take time to check gauge.

Ruby Red

Stitch Key

☐	K on RS, p on WS
—	P on RS, k on WS
◿	K2tog
◺	Ssk
⊙	Yo

Blanket

With circular needle, cast on 109 sts. Work 15 rows in moss st, end with a WS row.

Next row (RS) Keeping continuity of pattern, work 12 sts in moss st, pm, work row 1 of geometric pattern over next 85 sts, pm, work 12 st in moss st. Cont as now established, keeping first and last 12 sts in moss st, until rows 1–24 of geometric pattern have been worked 6 times, end with a WS row.

Next row (RS) Work in moss st across all sts. Work another 14 rows in moss st, end with a RS row. Bind off all sts in pattern.

Finishing

Weave in all ends. Block gently to measurements. ■

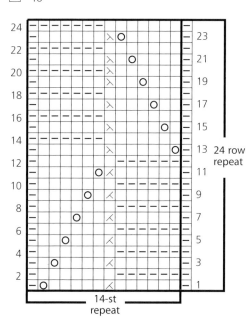

14-st repeat

24 row repeat

21

Stripe It Rich

For an easy knit that makes a big impact, work bright, multicolored stripes in garter stitch.

DESIGNED BY RENÉE LORION

Knitted Measurements
Approx 28" x 42"/71cm x 106.5cm

Materials
■ 1 3½oz/100g ball (each approx 220yd/200m) Cascade Yarns *220 Superwash* (superwash wool) each in #849 dark aqua (A), #827 coral (B), #808 sunset orange (C), #1973 seafoam heather (D), #821 daffodil (E), and #900 charcoal (F)

■ Size 7 (4.5mm) circular needle, 32"/80cm long, *or size to obtain gauge*

■ Size G/6 (4mm) crochet hook

Stripe Sequence
4 rows A, 3 rows B, 2 rows C, 6 rows D, 3 rows E, 2 rows B, 4 rows F, 8 rows A, 1 row B, 6 rows C, 4 rows D, 5 rows B, 3 rows E, 3 rows F.
Rep these 54 rows for stripe sequence.

Note
When possible, carry yarn up sides of work. Crochet edging is used to secure carried yarn and any ends.

Blanket
With F, cast on 170 sts. Work 6 rows in garter st (k every row).
Cont in garter st, work 54-row stripe sequence 4 times.
With F, k 3 rows. Bind off.

Finishing
With RS facing and crochet hook, work a row of sc along side edge, working one sc for every 2 rows and securing carried yarn in edging. Fasten off. Rep for opposite side edge. Weave in ends and block lightly to measurements. ■

Gauge
16 sts and 32 rows to 4"/10cm over garter st using size 7 (4.5mm) circular needle.
Take time to check gauge.

All About Aran

A moss stitch border frames a traditional cable pattern that looks fresh and modern in vibrant green.

DESIGNED BY DEBBIE O'NEILL

Knitted Measurements
Approx 31"x 37"/78.5cm x 94cm (36"x 48"/91.5cm x 122cm), after blocking
Instructions are written for small-size blanket. Changes for larger size are given in parentheses.

Materials
■ 6 (9) 3½oz/100g hanks (each approx 128yd/117m) of Cascade *128 Superwash* (superwash merino) in #802 green apple

■ Size 9 (5.5mm) circular needle, 36"/91cm long, *or size to obtain gauge*

■ Cable needle (cn)

Stitch Glossary
C6B Slip 3 sts to cn and hold to back, k3, k3 from cn.
C4B Slip 2 sts to cn and hold to back, k2, k2 from cn.
T3B Slip 1 st to cn and hold to back, k2, p1 from cn.
T3F Slip 2 sts to cn and hold to front, p1, k2 from cn.

Moss Stitch
Row 1 (WS) *K1, p1; rep from * to end.
Row 2 *K1, p1; rep from * to end.
Row 3 *P1, k1; rep from * to end.
Row 4 *P1, k1; rep from * to end.
Rep rows 1–4 for moss st.

Cable Pattern
Row 1 (WS) K2, p6, k2, *k4, p4, k6, p6, k2; rep from * to end.
Row 2 P2, C6B, p2, *p4, C4B, p6, C6B, p2; rep from * to end.
Row 3 K2, p6, k2, *k4, p4, k6, p6, k2; rep from * to end.
Row 4 P2, k6, p2, *p3, T3B, T3F, p5, k6, p2; rep from * to end.
Row 5 K2, p6, k2, *k3, p2, k2, p2, k5, p6, k2; rep from * to end.
Row 6 P2, k6, p2, *p2, T3B, p2, T3F, p4, k6, p2; rep from * to end.
Row 7 K2, p6, k2, *k2, p2, k4, p2, k4, p6, k2; rep from * to end.
Row 8 P2, k6, p2, *p2, k2, p4, k2, p4, k6, p2; rep from * to end.
Row 9 K2, p6, k2, *k2, p2, k4, p2, k4, p6, k2; rep from * to end.
Row 10 P2, k6, p2, *p2, T3F, p2, T3B, p4, k6, p2; rep from * to end.
Row 11 K2, p6, k2, *k3, p2, k2, p2, k5, p6, k2; rep from * to end.
Row 12 P2, k6, p2, *p3, T3F, T3B, p6, k5, p2; rep from * to end.
Rep rows 1–12 for cable pat.

Blanket
With circular needle, cast on 120 (140) sts. Work in moss st for 12 rows, ending with a RS row.
Set-up row (WS) Work in moss st for 6 sts, k2, p1, M1, p2, M1, p1, k2, *k4, p4, k6, p1, M1, p2, M1, p1, k2; rep from * 4 (5) times more, work last 6 sts in moss st—132 (154) sts. Work in cable pat, beg with row 2 and maintaining moss st borders as set, until piece measures approx 2"/5cm less than desired length, ending with row 3 of cable pat.
Next row (RS) Work in moss st, dec 12 (14) sts evenly across (dec 1 st at each end of each 6-st cable)—120 (140) sts. Work in moss st for 11 rows more. Bind off in pat.

Finishing
Weave in ends. Block lightly to measurements. ■

Gauges
14 sts and 20 rows = 4"/10cm over St st using size 9 (5.5mm) needle.
16 sts and 20 rows = 4"/10cm over pat st using size 9 (5.5mm) needle. *Take time to check gauges.*

Singing the Blues

Textured stripes knitted in a reverse rice stitch are soft on the eyes and soft on baby's skin.

DESIGNED BY LOIS S. YOUNG

Knitted Measurements
Approx 28½" x 34"/71cm x 86.5cm

Materials
- 3 3½oz/100g balls (each approx 220yd/200m) of Cascade Yarns *220 Superwash* (superwash wool) in #897 baby denim (A)
- 2 balls each in #884 skyline blue (B) and #813 blue velvet (C)
- Size 6 (4mm) circular needle, 36"/90cm long, *or size to obtain gauge*
- Two size 7 (4.5mm) double-pointed needles (dpns)
- Large-eye darning needle

Notes
1) Carry color not in use for 4 rows or less loosely up side of blanket, except for rows 5–22. When color isn't in use for more than 4 rows, cut yarn, leaving a long end for weaving in. When attaching I-cord edge, enclose carried-along yarn in I-cord.
2) Blanket is worked in rows. Circular needle is used to accommodate large number of sts—do not join.

Pattern Stitch
(over an even number of sts)
Row 1 (WS) Knit.
Row 2 *K1, p1, rep from *, end k1.
Repeat rows 1 and 2 for pat st.

Color Sequence
Rows 1–4 Work pat in C.
Rows 5 –12 Work pat in B.
Rows 13–22 Work pat in A.
Rows 23 and 24 Work pat in C.
Rows 25–28 Work pat in B.
Rows 29–32 Work pat in A.
Rep rows 1–32 for pat in color sequence.

Blanket
With C, loosely cast on 165 sts. Beg with a RS row, work 3 rows in pat. Beg with row 5, work in color sequence until row 32 is complete. Then work rows 1–32 of color sequence 7 times. With C, work 3 rows in pat as established. Bind off very loosely.

I-CORD EDGE
With dpn, cast on 4 sts. With WS of blanket facing, beg at one corner, *pick up and k 1 st from side of blanket, do not turn work, slide sts to opposite end of needle to work next row from RS, pull yarn firmly across back of I-cord sts, k3, k2tog; rep from * along side edge of blanket, skipping every 4th row, until entire side edge has been worked. Work 1 row without attaching to blanket edge, then [k2tog] twice and pass 1st st over 2nd and fasten off.
Rep for other side edge of blanket.

Finishing
Weave in ends. Block lightly to measurements. ■

Gauge
22 stitches and 32 rows to 4"/10cm square over pat st using size 6 (4mm) needle.
Take time to check gauge.

Building Blocks

Funky squares in a bright palette bring a geometric pizzazz to any nursery.

DESIGNED BY GALINA CARROLL

Knitted Measurements
Approx 23"/58.5cm square

Materials
■ 1 3½oz/100g hank (each approx 128yd/117m) of Cascade Yarns *128 Superwash* (superwash merino) each in #844 periwinkle (A), #821 daffodil (B), and #1964 cerise (C)

■ One pair size 10 (6mm) needles *or size to obtain gauge*

■ Size G/7 (4.5mm) crochet hook

■ Bobbins (optional)

Note
When changing colors, bring new color up from under old to avoid gaps. Wind yarn onto separate bobbins or small balls for easier handling.

Blanket
With A, cast on 38 sts; with C, cast on 19 sts; with B, cast on 19 sts. Work rows 1–58 of chart.

Next row Begin again at row 1 of chart, but reverse left and right halves as foll: work sts 39–76, then work sts 1–38. Continue to work chart through row 40, reversing left and right color blocks as established, beginning each row at st 39.

Finishing
Block to measurements. With crochet hook and C, work 1 rnd of sc around outside edge, followed by 1 rnd of dc. Fasten off. Weave in ends. ■

Gauge
13 sts and 20 rows to 4"/10cm over St st using size 10 (6mm) needles.
Take time to check gauge.

Building Blocks

57 55 53 51 49 47 45 43 41 39 37 35 33 31 29 27 25 23 21 19 17 15 13 11 9 7 5 3 1

1
10
20
30
38
40
50
60
70
76

58 56 54 52 50 48 46 44 42 40 38 36 34 32 30 28 26 24 22 20 18 16 14 12 10 8 6 4 2

Stitch Key

☐ RS: knit stitch, WS: purl stitch

▣ RS: purl stitch, WS: knit stitch

Hip to Be Square

An asymmetrical pattern of mitered squares is the height of cool in rich shades of blue.

DESIGNED BY STACEY GERBMAN

■■■□

Knitted Measurements
Approx 36½"/92.5cm square

Materials
■ 4 3½oz/100g balls (each approx 220yd/200m) Cascade Yarns *220 Superwash* (superwash wool) in #1973 seafoam heather (A)

■ 2 balls each in #1960 pacific (B) and #812 turquoise (C)

■ 1 ball in #856 aporto (D)

■ Size 7 (4.5mm) circular needle, 24"/60cm long, *or size to obtain gauge*

■ Stitch markers

Mitered Square (make 8)
With A, cast on 83 sts.
Row 1 (RS) Knit.
Row 2 (WS) K40, place marker, SK2P, k to end.
Row 3 (RS) Knit.
Row 4 (WS) Knit to 1 st before marker, place new marker, SK2P removing original marker, k to end.
Rep last 2 rows 12 times more. Cut A and join B.
Row 29 (RS) With B, knit.
Row 30 (WS) With B, rep row 4.
Rep last 2 rows 13 times more.
Cut B and join C.

Row 57 (RS) With C, knit.
Row 58 (WS) With C, rep row 4.
Rep last 2 rows 11 times more, then rep row 57 once more.
Row 82 SK2P, cut yarn and pull through last st.

Joined Mitered Squares (make 4)
Place two mitered squares with C corners touching (see joining diagram). With A and RS facing, beg at corner 1 and, working toward corner 2, *pick up 41 sts along edge of first mitered square, cast on 1 st in corner, pick up 41 sts along edge of second mitered square 83 sts. Beg with row 2, finish as for mitered square. Rep from * with A and RS facing, beg at corner 3 and picking up along lower and side edges of squares to corner 4.

Finishing
With RS facing, sew joined mitered squares tog according to placement diagram.

Gauge
19 sts and 39 rows to 4"/10cm over garter st using size 7 (4.5mm) needles.
Take time to check gauge.

Hip to Be Square

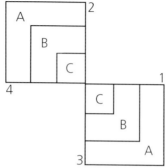

JOINING DIAGRAM

EDGING

With RS facing and D, pick up and knit 164 sts along side edge of blanket. K 12 rows. Bind off. Rep for opposite side edge.

With RS facing and D, pick up and knit 7 sts along top edge of border, 164 sts along top edge of blanket, 7 sts along top edge of opposite border 178 sts. K 12 rows. Bind off. Rep for lower edge. Weave in all ends. Block lightly to measurements. ■

PLACEMENT DIAGRAM

26

Catty-Corner

An easy garter-stitch blanket makes a statement with bold colors and graphic stripes knit on the diagonal.

DESIGNED BY CAROL SULCOSKI

Knitted Measurements
Approx 30"/76cm square

Materials
■ 4 3½oz/100g balls (each approx 220yd/201m) Cascade Yarns *220 Superwash* (superwash wool) in #808 sunset orange (A)

■ 1 ball in #805 violet (B)

■ Size 8 (5mm) circular needle, 32"/80cm long, *or size to obtain gauge*

Notes
1) Blanket is worked diagonally.
2) Blanket is worked back and forth in rows. Circular needle is used to accommodate large number of sts—do not join.
3) Blanket edges are left as knit. Do not carry yarn along side edge of work.

Stripe Pattern
Working in garter st (knit every row) throughout, work 32 rows A, [2 rows B, 6 rows A] twice, 2 rows B, 30 rows A, [2 rows B, 12 rows A] twice, 2 rows B, 72 rows A, [8 rows B, 2 rows A] twice, 8 rows B, 72 rows A, [4 rows B, 12 rows A] twice, 4 rows B, 30 rows A, [2 rows B, 6 rows A] twice, 2 rows B, 32 rows A.

Blanket
With MC, cast on 3 sts. Following stripe pat, proceed as follows:
Row 1 (inc) (RS) Kf&b, k1, kf&b—5 sts.
Row 2 Knit.
Row 3 Kf&b, k to last st, kf&b—7 sts.
Row 4 Knit.
Continue as established, following stripe pat, repeating last 2 rows until there are 205 sts on needle; end with a WS row.
Next (dec) row (RS) K2tog, k to last 2 sts, k2tog.
Next row Knit.
Keeping continuity of stripe pat, repeat last 2 rows until there are 3 sts on needle; end with a WS row.
Bind off rem 3 sts.

Finishing
Weave in ends. Block to finished measurements. ■

Gauge
19 sts and 38 rows to 4"/10cm over garter st using size 8 (5mm) circular needle.
Take time to check gauge.

Googly-Eyed Gator

A softly scaly friend rests on a bed of stripes in this showstopper.
Use it as a blanket or to decorate the nursery!

DESIGNED BY ASHLEY RAO

Knitted Measurements
Approx 38" x 42"/96.5cm x 106.5cm

Materials
■ 4 3½oz/100g balls (each approx 220yd/200m) Cascade Yarns *220 Superwash* (superwash wool) each in #892 space needle (A) and #817 aran (B)

■ 3 balls in #887 wasabi (C)

■ One size 6 (4mm) circular needle, 40"/100cm long, *or size to obtain gauge*

■ One set (5) size 6 (4mm) double-pointed needles (dpns)

■ Two 1¼"/32mm buttons

■ Polyfill stuffing

■ Stitch markers

Stitch Glossary
MB (make bobble) K4, [turn, sl 1 purlwise, p3, turn, sl 1 knitwise, k3] 4 times.

Notes
1) Circular needle is used to accommodate large number of sts—do not join.
2) When changing colors, twist yarns to eliminate holes. If color shifts more than 3 sts, break and rejoin yarn.
3) Charts show only RS rows. Work WS rows even by working colors as shown in previous RS row.

Blanket
With A, cast on 200 sts. Work 20 rows in garter st (k every row). Cut A and change to B.
With B, k 4 rows.
BEG TAIL
Row 25 (RS) With B, k97; with C, k52. With B, k to end.
Next row and all WS rows Knit B sts in B and C sts in C.
Row 27 With B, k87; with C, k65; with B, k to end.
Row 29 With B, k77; with C, k77; with B, k to end.

Row 31 With B, k67; with C, k89; with B, k to end.
Row 33 With B, k57; with C, k43; *MB, k1; rep from * 8 times, k12; with B, k to end.
Row 35 With B, k47; with C, k111; with B, k to end.
Row 37 With B, k37; with C, k122; with B, k to end.
Row 39 With B, k27; with C, k132; with B, k to end.
Row 40 Knit B sts in B and C sts in C. Cut B and join A.
Row 41 With A, k17; with C, k48; *MB, k1; rep from * 17 times, k5; with A, k to end.
Row 42 and all WS rows Knit A sts in A and C sts in C.
Row 43 With A, k14; with C, k146; with A, k to end.
Row 45 With A, k13; with C, k148; with A, k to end.
Row 47 With A, k12; with C, k149; with A, k to end.
Row 49 With A, k11; with C, k4; *MB, k1; rep from * 27 times, k7; with A, k to end.
Row 51 With A, k10; with C, k152; with A, k to end.

Gauge
19 sts and 40 rows = 4"/10cm over garter st using size 6 (4mm) needles.
Take time to check gauge.

Googly-Eyed Gator

CHART A

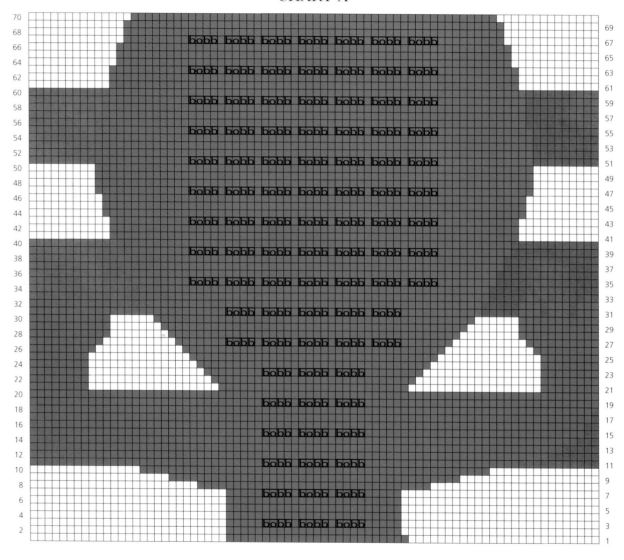

- ■ Space Needle (A)
- □ Aran (B)
- ■ Wasabi (C)
- **bobb** 4-st bobble

CHART B

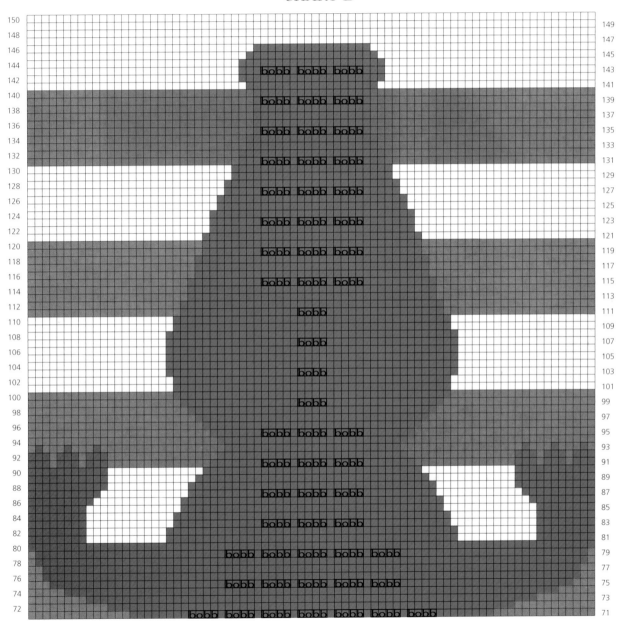

Googly-Eyed Gator

27

TAIL CHART

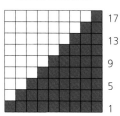

Rows 53 and 55 With A, k10; with C, k152; with A, k to end.
Row 57 With A, k10; with C, k135; *MB, k1; rep from * 2 times, k3; with A, k to end.
Row 59 With A, k10; with C, k153; with A, k to end.
Row 60 Knit A sts in A and C sts in C.

BEG TAIL CHART AND BODY CHART
Row 61 With B, k10; work 9 sts of tail chart; with B, k94, pm, work 78 sts of body chart, pm; with B, work to end.
Row 62 and all WS rows Knit B sts in B and C sts in C.
Cont to work charts in this way through row 18 of tail chart, then work as foll:
Row 79 With B, k to marker, work 78 sts of body chart; with B, k to end.
Row 80 Work even. Cut B.
Row 81 With A, k to marker, work 78 sts of body chart; with A, k to end.
Cont to work body chart between markers in this way, working the sts outside of markers as foll: *20 rows A, 20 rows B; rep from * to end of chart. With A, k 20 rows. Bind off.

EYES
With dpn and B, cast on 8 sts, leaving a long tail. Evenly divide sts so there are 2 on each needle. Join and place marker (pm) for beg of rnd, taking care not to twist sts.
Rnd 1 Knit.
Rnd 2 (inc) *M1, k to last st on needle, M1, k1; rep from * around 8 sts inc'd. Rep last 2 rnds 3 times more—40 sts. Knit 2 rnds.
Next rnd (dec) *K2tog, k to last 2 sts on needle, k2tog; rep from * around 8 sts dec'd.
Next rnd Knit.
Rep last 2 rnds 2 times more, then rep dec rnd once more 8 sts. Cut yarn, leaving long tail.
Thread tail through rem sts, fill eye with stuffing. Draw tail up to close sts and secure.
Thread tail from cast-on through center of eyeball to shape. Secure eyeballs to blanket. Sew buttons to eyeballs, using photograph as guide.

Finishing
Weave in all ends. Block lightly to measurements. ■

Window Dressing

Peek-a-boo! Two columns of leaves in a lighter hue pop out of the center to make an eye-catching blanket.

DESIGNED BY TABETHA HEDRICK

Knitted Measurements
Approx 34" x 33.5"/86.5cm x 85cm

Materials
- 4 3½oz/100g balls (each approx 220yd/200m) of Cascade Yarns *220 Superwash* (superwash wool) in #857 brambleberry (MC)
- 1 ball in #840 iris (CC)
- Size 8 (5mm) circular needle, 24"/61cm long, *or size to obtain gauge*
- 2 size 8 (5mm) double-pointed needles (dpns)
- Size 8/H (5mm) crochet hook
- Waste yarn

Note
When working the leaf motif section, cross the new yarn under the old yarn before working with it, to firm up the intarsia edge.

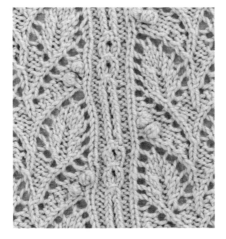

Stitch Glossary
k3tog Knit 3 stitches together.
MB (make bobble) With crochet hook, (k, yo, k, yo, k) in next st; then yo and draw yo through 5 sts. Insert hook into st below, yo, pull through st, pass the last st over the yo and transfer st to RH needle.
wrap 3 Insert RH needle into third st on LH needle and draw this st over first 2 sts on LH needle and off the needle; k1, yo, k1.
wrap 3 tbl Insert RH needle into third st on LH needle and draw this st over first 2 sts on LH needle and off the needle; k1 tbl, yo, k1 tbl.

Seed Stitch
(over odd number of sts)
Row 1 P1, *k1, p1; rep from * across.
Repeat row 1 for seed st.

Leaf Motif
(over 47 sts)
Row 1 (RS) K1 tbl, p2, k1, yo, k5, yo, SK2P, p2, k2tog, yo, p2, MB, k1, p2, k3, p2, k1, yo, k5, yo, SK2P, p2, k2tog, yo, p2, MB, k1, p2, k1 tbl.
Row 2 P1 tbl, k2, p1, k4, p1, k2, p9, k2, p3, k2, p1, k4, p1, k2, p9, k2, p1 tbl.
Row 3 K1 tbl, p2, k1, yo, k1, ssk, p1, k2tog, k1, yo, k1, p1, k2tog, yo, p2, MB, p1, k1, p2, wrap 3 tbl, p2, k1, yo, k1, ssk, p1, k2tog, k1, yo, k1, p1, k2tog, yo, p2, MB, p1, k1, p2, k1 tbl.
Row 4 P1 tbl, k2, p2, k4, p1, k1, p4, k1, p4, k2, p1 tbl, k1 tbl, p1 tbl, k2, p2, k4, p1, k1, p4, k1, p4, k2, p1 tbl.
Row 5 K1 tbl, p2, k1, yo, k1, ssk, p1, k2tog, k1, yo, k1, k2tog, yo, p3, k2tog, yo, k1, p2, k1 tbl, p1, k1 tbl, p2, k1, yo, k1, ssk, p1, k2tog, k1, yo, k1, k2tog, yo, p3, k2tog, yo, k1, p2, k1 tbl.

Gauges
18 sts and 32 rows to 4"/10cm in seed st using size 8 (5mm) circular needle.
18 sts and 30 rows to 4"/10cm in leaf motif using size 8 (5mm) circular needle. *Take time to check gauges.*

Row 6 P1 tbl, k2, p3, k4, [p2, k1] 3 times, p1, k2, p1 tbl, k1, p1 tbl, k2, p3, k4, [p2, k1] 3 times, p1, k2, p1 tbl.

Row 7 K1 tbl, p2, k1, p1, yo, ssk, p1, k2tog, yo, p1, k2tog, yo, p2, k3tog, yo, k1, yo, k1, p2, k1 tbl, p1, k1 tbl, p2, k1, p1, yo, ssk, p1, k2tog, yo, p1, k2tog, yo, p2, k3tog, yo, k1, yo, k1, p2, k1 tbl.

Row 8 P1 tbl, k2, p5, k3, p1, k2, p1, k1, [p1, k2] twice, p1 tbl, k1, p1 tbl, k2, p5, k3, p1, k2, p1, k1, [p1, k2] twice, p1 tbl.

Row 9 K1 tbl, p2, k1, p2, yo, SK2P, yo, p2, k1, p1, k3tog, yo, k3, yo, k1, p2, k1 tbl, p1, k1 tbl, p2, k1, p2, yo, SK2P, yo, p2, k1, p1, k3tog, yo, k3, yo, k1, p2, k1 tbl.

Row 10 P1 tbl, k2, p7, k1, [p1, k3] twice, p1, k2, p1 tbl, k1, p1 tbl, k2, p7, k1, [p1, k3] twice, p1, k2, p1 tbl.

Row 11 K1 tbl, p2, k1, MB, p2, yo, ssk, p2, k3tog, yo, k5, yo, k1, p2, k1 tbl, p1, k1 tbl, p2, k1, MB, p2, yo, ssk, p2, k3tog, yo, k5, yo, k1, p2, k1 tbl.

Row 12 P1 tbl, k2, p9, k2, p1, k4, p1, k2, p1 tbl, k1, p1 tbl, k2, p9, k2, p1, k4, p1, k2, p1 tbl.

Row 13 K1 tbl, p2, k1, p1, MB, p2, yo, ssk, p1, k1, yo, k1, ssk, p1, k2tog, k1, yo, k1, p2, k1 tbl, p1, k1 tbl, p2, k1, p1, MB, p2, yo, ssk, p1, k1, yo, k1, ssk, p1, k2tog, k1, yo, k1, p2, k1 tbl.

Row 14 P1 tbl, k2, [p4, k1] twice, p1, k4, p2, k2, p1 tbl, k1, p1 tbl, k2, [p4, k1] twice, p1, k4, p2, k2, p1 tbl.

Row 15 K1 tbl, p2, k1, yo, ssk, p3, yo, ssk, k1, yo, k1, ssk, p1, k2tog, k1, yo, k1, p2, wrap 3, p2, k1, yo, ssk, p3, yo, ssk,

k1, yo, k1, ssk, p1, k2tog, k1, yo, k1, p2, k1 tbl.

Row 16 P1 tbl, k2, p1, k1, [p2, k1] twice, p2, k4, p3, k2, p3, k2, p1, k1, [p2, k1] twice, p2, k4, p3, k2, p1 tbl.

Row 17 K1 tbl, p2, [k1, yo] twice, SK2P, p2, [yo, ssk, p1] twice, k2tog, yo, p1, k1, p2, k3, p2, [k1, yo] twice, SK2P, p2, [yo, ssk, p1] twice, k2tog, yo, p1, k1, p2, k1 tbl.

Row 18 P1 tbl, [k2, p1] twice, k1, p1, k2, p1, k3, p5, k2, p3, [k2, p1] twice, k1, p1, k2, p1, k3, p5, k2, p1 tbl.

Row 19 K1 tbl, p2, k1, yo, k3, yo, SK2P, p1, k1, p2, yo, k3tog, yo, p2, k1, p2, wrap 3, p2, k1, yo, k3, yo, SK2P, p1, k1, p2, yo, k3tog, yo, p2, k1, p2, k1 tbl.

Row 20 P1 tbl, k2, [p1, k3] twice, p1, k1, p7, k2, p3, k2, [p1, k3] twice, p1, k1, p7, k2, p1 tbl.

Blanket
BOTTOM BORDER
With MC and circular needle, cast on 153 sts. Beg seed st and work even for 87 rows, or until piece measures 11"/28cm from cast-on edge, ending with a RS row.

LEAF PANEL
Row 1 (WS) Work even in seed st for 53 sts, join CC and p47, join MC and work even in seed st for 53 sts. Each side section is worked at the same time.
Next row (RS) Work seed st in MC for 53 sts, change to CC and work leaf motif row 1, change to MC and work seed st to end. Cont working blanket as established through row 20 of leaf motif. Repeat rows 1–20 three more times, ending with a WS row.

TOP BORDER
Change to MC.
Next row (RS) Work 53 sts in seed st, k47, work 53 sts in seed st.
Row 2 Work seed st to end.
Continue in seed st for 86 more rows, or until MC top border measures 11"/28cm from last row of leaf motif, ending with a WS row. Bind off loosely.

Finishing
Weave in ends. Block piece to measurements.

ATTACHED I-CORD EDGING
Note When picking up sts around blanket, pick up 1 st for every bound-off or cast-on st, and on selvedge edge, pick up 3 sts for every 4 rows.

Using provisional cast-on, dpns, and waste yarn, cast on 4 sts. Beg at lower RH corner of blanket, with CC, work as foll: *K3, s1, yo, pick up and k 1 st from blanket, pass the yo and slipped st over the picked-up st. Push the sts to right end of dpns; rep from * until all edges of blanket have been worked and you are back at the beg. Place sts from provisional I-cord cast-on onto dpns and graft ends together using kitchener st. ∎

Lacy Chevron

A generous-size crib blanket wraps baby in a pretty combination of solids and heathers.

DESIGNED BY REBECCA KLASSEN

■■■□

Knitted Measurements
Approx 35"x 44"/89cm x 111.5cm

Materials
■ 2 3½oz/100g balls (each approx 220yd/200m) of Cascade Yarns *220 Superwash Quatro* (superwash wool) each in #1931 summerdaze (A), #1928 oceanside (B), #1930 green tea (C), and #1932 butterscotch (D)

■ Size 6 (4mm) circular needle, 32"/80cm long, *or size to obtain gauge*

Pattern Stitch
(multiple of 18 sts plus 26)
Row 1 (RS) K5, yo, *k6, k2tog, SKP, k6, yo, k2; rep from * to last 21 sts, k6, SKP, k2tog, k6, yo, k5.
Row 2 Sl 4 wyif, p to last 4 sts, sl 4 wyif.
Rows 3–10 Rep rows 1 and 2 four times more.
Row 11 K5, yo, *p6, p2tog tbl, p2tog, p6, yo, k2, yo; rep from * to last 21 sts, p6, p2tog tbl, p2tog, p6, yo, k5.
Row 12 Sl 4 wyif, p1, *k16, p2; rep from * to last 21 sts, k16, p1, sl 4. Rep rows 1–12 for pat st.

Note
Piece is worked in stripes in a chevron pattern, with slipped stitches at each side that form an I-cord edging.

Blanket
With A, cast on 188 sts.
Border row 1 (RS) Knit.
Border row 2 Sl 4 wyif, p to last 4 sts, sl 4 wyif. Rep border rows 1 and 2 once more. Beg pat st. *Work rows 1–12 of pat st 3 times; rep from * in color sequence as foll: A, B, C, D, A, B, C. With D, work rows 1–12 of pat st twice, then rep rows 1–11 twice.
Next row Sl 4 wyif, p to last 4 sts, sl 4.
Next row K5, p to last 5 sts, k5.
Next row Bind off purlwise.

Finishing
Weave in ends. Block lightly to measurements. ■

Gauge
22 sts and 24 rows to 4"/10cm using size 6 (4mm) circular needle over pattern stitch.
Take time to check gauge.

Pumpkin Patch

An easy garter rib blanket becomes something special when it's knit in warm stripes of autumnal orange.

DESIGNED BY THERESE CHYNOWETH

Knitted Measurements
Approx 36"/91.5cm square

Materials
■ 4 3.5oz/100g balls (each approx 220yd/201m) of Cascade Yarns *220 Superwash* (superwash wool) in #826 tangerine (MC)

■ 2 balls in #1976 sunshine heather (CC)

■ Size 7 (4.5mm) circular needle, 32"/81cm long, *or size to obtain gauge*

Notes
1) Blanket is worked back and forth in rows. Circular needle is used to accommodate large number of sts—do not join.
2) Blanket edges are left as knit. Carry yarn not in use neatly along side edge of work.

Garter Rib Pattern
(multiple of 6 sts plus 3)
Rows 1 and 3 (RS) With MC, k4, *p1, k5; rep from * to last 5 sts, p1, k4.
Rows 2 and 4 With MC, *k3, p1, k1, p1; rep from * to last 3 sts, k3.
Rows 5 and 7 With CC, k4, *p1, k5; rep from * to last 5 sts, p1, k4.
Rows 6 and 8 With CC, *k3, p1, k1, p1; rep from * to last 3 sts, k3.
Rep rows 1–8 for garter rib pat.

Blanket
With MC, cast on 189 sts. Work even in garter rib pat until piece measures approx 36"/91.5cm from beg, end with row 4 of pat. Bind off in pat.

Finishing
Weave in all ends. Block lightly to measurements. ■

Gauge
21 sts and 30 rows to 4"/10cm over garter rib pat using size 7 (4.5mm) circular needle.
Take time to check gauge.

Blue Diamonds

An allover argyle stitch pattern makes a plush and eye-catching statement in little-boy blue.

DESIGNED BY AMANDA BLAIR BROWN

◼◼◻◻

Knitted Measurements
Approx 32" x 40"/81cm x 101.5cm

Materials
- 8 3½oz/100g hanks (each approx 128yd/117m) Cascade Yarns *128 Superwash* (superwash merino) in #896 blue horizon
- Size 9 (5.5mm) circular needle, 32"/80cm long, *or size to obtain gauge*

Argyle Pattern
(over multiple of 8 sts)

Row 1 (WS) Sl 1, *p6, k2; rep from * to last 7 sts, p7.

Row 2 (RS) Sl 1, *k6, p2; rep from * to last 7 sts, k7.

Row 3 Sl 1, *k1, p4, k1, p2; rep from * to last 7 sts, k1, p4, k1, p1.

Row 4 Sl 1, *p1, k4, p1, k2; rep from * to last 7 sts, p1, k4, p1, k1.

Row 5 Sl 1, p1, *k1, p2, k1, p4; rep from * to last 6 sts, k1, p2, k1, p2.

Row 6 Sl 1, k1, *p1, k2, p1, k4; rep from * to last 6 sts, p1, k2, p1, k2.

Row 7 Sl 1, p2, *k2, p6; rep from * to last 5 sts, k2, p3.

Row 8 Sl 1, k2, *p2, k6; rep from * to last 5 sts, p2, k3.

Row 9 Rep row 7.

Row 10 Rep row 8.

Row 11 Rep row 5.

Row 12 Rep row 6.

Row 13 Rep row 3.

Row 14 Rep row 4.

Row 15 Rep row 1.

Row 16 Rep row 2.

Rep rows 1–16 for argyle pat.

Note
Circular needle is used to accommodate large number of sts—do not join.

Blanket
Cast on 142 sts.

Row 1 (WS) Knit.

Row 2 (RS) K1, k2tog, k to last 3 sts, k2tog, k1—2 sts dec'd.

Rep last 2 rows twice more—136 sts.

BEG ARGYLE PAT

Work rows 1–16 of argyle pat 13 times.

Next row (WS) Knit.

Next row (RS) K1, M1, k to last st, M1, k1—2 sts inc'd.

Rep last 2 rows twice more—142 sts. Bind off.

EDGING

With RS facing, pick up and k 170 sts along side edge.

Row 1 (WS) Knit.

Row 2 (RS) K1, M1, k to last st, M1, k1—2 sts inc'd.

Row 3 (WS) Knit.

Rep last 2 rows once, then rep row 1 once more—176 sts. Bind off. Rep for opposite side edge.

Finishing
Sew side edges of garter borders at corners. Weave in all ends. Block lightly to measurements. ◼

Gauge
18 sts and 22 rows to 4"/10cm over argyle pat using size 9 (5.5mm) needles.
Take time to check gauge.

Fetching Fibonacci

A spiral of increasingly larger blocks based on the Fibonacci sequence makes an easy-to-knit but stunning modern statement.

DESIGNED BY FAITH HALE

Knitted Measurements
Approx 23" x 28½"/58.5cm x 72.5cm

Materials
- 2 3½oz/100g balls (each approx 220yd/201m) of Cascade Yarns *220 Superwash* (superwash wool) each in #824 yellow (E) and #1915 banana cream (F)
- 1 ball each in #1952 blaze (A), #825 orange (B), #877 golden (C), and #821 daffodil (D)
- Size 7 (4.5mm) circular needle, 36"/90cm long, *or size to obtain gauge*
- Size H/8 (5mm) crochet hook
- Scrap yarn (approx 2yd/2m in contrasting color)
- Stitch markers

Notes
1) Blanket is worked back and forth in rows. Circular needle is used to accommodate large number of sts—do not join.
2) Pick up and knit sts between the garter st ridges along the marked side edges.

Provisional Cast-on
Using scrap yarn and crochet hook, ch the number of sts to cast on plus a few extra. Cut a tail and pull the tail through the last chain. With knitting needle and yarn, pick up and knit the stated number of sts through the "purl bumps" on the back of the chain. To remove scrap yarn chain, when instructed, pull out the tail from the last crochet stitch. Gently and slowly pull on the tail to unravel the crochet stitches, carefully placing each released knit stitch on a needle.

Blanket
A
Using provisional cast-on and A, cast on 9 sts. Work 36 rows in garter st (k every row). With RS facing, place marker (pm) in LH edge of work. Cut yarn and place sts on a length of scrap yarn.
B
With RS facing and B, pick up and k 17 sts along marked edge of piece A. Work 34 rows in garter st. With RS facing, pm in LH edge of work. Cut yarn and place sts on a length of scrap yarn.
C
With RS facing and C, pick up and k 16 sts along marked edge of piece B. Carefully remove provisional cast-on of piece A and knit the 9 sts—25 sts. Work 50 rows in garter st. With RS facing, pm in LH edge. Bind off.
D
With RS facing and D, pick up and k 42 sts along the marked edge of piece C and adjacent edge of piece A. Work 84 rows in garter st. With RS facing, pm in LH edge. Bind off.
E
With RS facing and E, pick up and k 64 sts along marked edge of piece D and adjacent edges of pieces A and B. Work 128 rows in garter st. With RS facing, pm in LH edge of piece E. Bind off.
F
With RS facing and F, pick up and k 62 sts along the marked edge of piece E. Carefully remove provisional cast-on from piece B and k those 17 sts, then pick up and k 24 sts along the adjacent edge of piece B—103 sts. Work 128 rows in garter stitch. Bind off.

Finishing
With RS facing, crochet hook, and D, sc around entire edge of blanket, working 1sc in each st on the short edges and 1sc in every other st on the long edges. Weave in ends and block lightly to measurements. ■

Gauge
18 sts and 36 rows to 4"/10cm over garter st using size 7 (4.5mm) circular needle.
Take time to check gauge.

Making Waves

Delicate waves of lace bordered in a bright-pink ruffle are the epitome of little-girl style.

DESIGNED BY JILL WRIGHT

Knitted Measurements
Blanket without ruffle 33.5" x 36"/85cm x 91.5cm
Ruffle 1.25"/3cm before bind-off

Materials
■ 7 3.5oz/100g balls (each approx 220yd/200m) of Cascade Yarns *220 Superwash* (superwash wool) in #894 strawberry cream (MC)

■ 2 balls in #914A tahitian rose (CC)

■ One pair size 7 (4.5mm) needles, *or size to obtain gauge*

■ Size 7 (4.5mm) circular needle, 72"/182.5cm long

Notes
1) Center of blanket is worked flat in lacy wave pattern.
2) Ruffle is picked up around edge and worked out, increasing in purl sections only. Purl or knit all edge sts as required.

Stitch Glossary
M1P Insert LH needle from front to back under bar between sts, purl through back loop.

Lacy Wave Pattern
(multiple of 24 sts)
Rows 1, 3, 5, 7 P3, *yo, k4, k2tog, *p2, ktbl twice, p2; rep from * to * once, p3.
Rows 2, 4, 6, 8 K3, p6, k2, ptbl twice, k2, p6, k3.
Rows 9, 11, 13, 15 P3, *ssk, k4, yo, *p2, ktbl twice, p2; rep from * to * once, p3.
Rows 10, 12, 14, 16 Rep row 2.
Rep rows 1–16 for lacy wave pat.

Picot Bind-off
*(K1, sl st back to LH needle) twice, k2, sl first st over second st, sl rem st back to LH needle; rep from * around.

Blanket
With MC, cast on 192 sts.
Work in lacy wave pat until blanket measures 36"/91.5 cm from cast-on, do not bind off.

RUFFLE
Switch to circular needle and CC. With RS facing, knit 192, turn blanket, working along side edge pick up 164 sts, turn blanket, pick up 192 sts along cast-on edge, turn blanket, working along side edge pick up 164 sts—712 sts. Pm for beg of rnd. Work 1 rnd.
Rnd 1 Switch to MC, *K2, M1P; rep from * around—1,068 sts.
Rnd 2 *K2, p1; rep from * around.
Rnd 3 *K2, M1P, p1; rep from * around—1,424 sts.
Rnd 4 *K2, p2; rep from * around.
Rnd 5 *K2, p1, M1P, p1; rep from * around—1,780 sts.
Rnd 6 *K2, p3; rep from * around.
Rnd 7 *K2, p1, M1P, p2; rep from * around—2,136 sts.
Rnd 8 *K2, p4; rep from * around.
Work picot bind-off with CC.

Finishing
Weave in all ends. Block lightly to measurements. ■

Gauge
23 sts and 27 rows to 4"/10cm in lacy wave pattern (blocked) using size 7 (4.5mm) needle.
Take time to check gauge.

Team Colors

Get into the game-day spirit by making this striped and textured blanket in your favorite team's colors.

DESIGNED BY LISA SILVERMAN

Knitted Measurements
Approx 29"x 30"/73.5cm x 76cm

Materials
■ 2 3½oz/100g hanks (each approx 128yd/117m) of Cascade Yarns *128 Superwash* (superwash merino) each in #1951 sapphire heather (B) and #802 green apple (C)

■ 1 hank in #817 ecru (A)

■ Size 10 (6mm) circular needle, 32"/80cm long, *or size to obtain gauge*

Note
First and last 4 sts should be knit in seed st throughout. Instructions do not include these border sts.

Seed Stitch
Row 1 (RS) *K1, p1; rep from * to end.
Row 2 (WS) *P1, k1; rep from * to end.
Repeat rows 1 and 2 for seed st.

Blanket
With C, cast on 100 sts.
Rows 1–4 With C, work in seed st.
Row 5 (RS) Join A, knit.
Row 6 Purl.
Row 7 Join B, knit.
Row 8 *P4, k4; rep from * to last 4 sts before seed st border, end p4.
Row 9 *K4, p4; rep from * to last 4 sts before seed st border, end k4.
Rows 10 and 11 Rep rows 8 and 9 once more.
Row 12 Purl.
Row 13 Join A, knit.
Row 14 Purl.
Row 15 Join C, knit.
Row 16 *K2, p2; rep from * to end.
Row 17 *K2, p2; rep from * to end.
Row 18 Purl.
Row 19 Join B, knit.
Row 20 Purl.
Row 21 *K2, p8; rep from * to last 2 sts before border, end k2.
Row 22 *P2, k8; rep from * to last 2 sts before border, end p2.

Row 23 *K2, p2, k4, p2; rep from * to last 2 sts before border, end k2.
Row 24 *P2, k2, p4, k2; rep from * to last 2 sts before border, end p2.
Rows 25–28 Rep rows 23 and 24 twice more.
Row 29 *K2, p8; rep from * to last 2 sts before border, end k2.
Row 30 *P2, k8; rep from * to last 2 sts before border, end p2.
Row 31 Knit.
Row 32 Purl.
Rows 33–36 Join C, rep rows 15–18
Rows 37–46 Rep rows 5–14.
Row 47 Join C, knit.
Row 48 *K2, p2; rep from * to end.
Row 49 *K2, p2; rep from * to end.
Row 50 *P2, k2; rep from * to end.
Row 51 *P2, k2; rep from * to end.
Rows 52–55 Rep rows 48–51.
Row 56 *K2, p2; rep from * to end.
Row 57 *K2, p2; rep from * to end.
Row 58 Purl.
Rep rows 5–58 once more.
Rep rows 5–46 once.
Join C, work 4 rows in seed st.
Bind off.

Finishing
Weave in ends. Block lightly to measurements. ■

Gauge
19 sts and 26 rows to 4"/10cm over St st using size 10 (6mm) circular needle.
Take time to check gauge.

Tweedle-Dee

A tweedy slip-stitch pattern makes a dense, warm blanket that looks ultra cool in a palette of blues and greens.

DESIGNED BY THERESE CHYNOWETH

Knitted Measurements
Approx 29" x 35"/73.5cm x 89cm

Materials
■ 2 3½oz/100g balls (each approx 220yd/200m) of Cascade Yarns *220 Superwash* (superwash wool) each in #811 como blue (MC), #1985 duck egg blue (A), and #1942 mint (B).

■ Size 7 (4.5mm) circular needle, 32" long, *or size to obtain gauge*

■ Size E/4 (3.5mm) crochet hook

Note
On each RS row, begin by picking up the bottom-most color yarn and carrying it up the side to work with it. When the crocheted edging is applied, all the carries will be covered.

Blanket
With MC, very loosely cast on 149 stitches.
Purl one row.
Row 1 With A, *k1, sl 1 wyif, rep from *; end k1.
Rows 2, 4, 6, 8, 10, and 12 Purl.

Row 3 With B, k1, *k1, sl 1 wyif, rep from *; end k2.
Row 5 With MC, rep row 1.
Row 7 With A, rep row 3.
Row 9 With B, rep row 1.
Row 11 With MC, rep row 3.
Rep rows 1–12 until blanket measures 34"/86.5cm, ending with row 5. Cast off purlwise with MC; do not break yarn.

Finishing
CROCHET EDGING
Using last lp from cast-off, crochet hook, and RS facing, ch 1, sc 134 sts across top of blanket, sc 3 times into corner, sc 154 down side of blanket, sc 3 times into corner, sc 134 stitches across bottom of blanket, sc 3 times into corner, sc 154 up side of blanket, sc 3 times into corner and sl st to first sc in row. Ch 1, sc around, working 3 sc into each corner. Join with a sl st to first sc. Turn work, ch 1, and with wrong side facing work 1 rnd of reverse sc around entire edge. Join with a sl st to first rev sc. Finish off. Weave in ends and block lightly to measurements. ■

Gauges
20 sts and 34 rows to 4"/10cm in slipped stitch pattern using size 7 (4.5mm) needle.
18 sc to 4"/10cm using size E/4 (3.5mm) crochet hook. *Take time to check gauges.*

Eat Play Love

A motto for any baby to live by! The cheerful yellow background makes this a room-brightener in every way.

DESIGNED BY LAURA MALLER

Knitted Measurements
Approx 33½" x 39½"/85cm x 100.5cm

Materials
- 5 3½oz/100g balls (each approx 220yd/201m) Cascade Yarns *220 Superwash* (superwash wool) in #877 golden (MC)
- 2 balls in #1946 silver grey (A)
- 1 ball in #1913 jet (B)
- Size 6 (4mm) circular needle, 32"/80cm long, *or size to obtain gauge*

Garter Slip Stitch Pattern
(over an odd number of sts)
Rows 1 and 2 Knit.
Row 3 (RS) K1, *sl 1, k1; rep from * to end of row.
Row 4 K1, *sl 1 wyif, k1 wyib; rep from * to end of row.
Rows 5 and 6 Knit.
Row 7 K2, *sl 1, k1; rep from * to last st, k1.
Row 8 K2, *sl 1 wyif, k1 wyib; rep from * to last st, k1.
Rep rows 1–8 for garter slip st pat.

Stripe Pattern
*[2 rows A, 2 rows MC] twice, [2 rows MC, 2 rows A] twice; rep from * once more.

Note
Blanket is worked back and forth in rows. Circular needle is used to accommodate large number of sts—do not join.

Blanket
With B, cast on 130 sts. Work 4 rows in garter st (knit every row). Break B and join MC. Starting with a knit (RS) row, work even in St st until piece measures 30"/76cm from beg, end with a WS row. Break MC and join B. Work 4 rows in garter st. Bind off all sts knitwise.
With B, using photo as a guide, duplicate stitch "EAT PLAY LOVE" following charts, placing first letter approx 3 ½"/9cm in from side edge and 6½"/16.5cm down from top of blanket, with the words spaced approx 3"/7.5cm apart.

SIDE BORDER (MAKE 2)
With B, cast on 173 sts. Work 4 rows in garter st, end with a WS row. Break B and join A. Following stripe sequence, work in garter slip st pattern to end of stripe sequence, end with a WS row. With A, knit 2 rows. Bind off knitwise.

TOP/BOTTOM BORDER (MAKE 2)
With A, cast on 179 sts. Following stripe pat, work in garter slip st pat to end of stripe pat, end with a WS row. Break MC and A, leaving sts on needle.
With right side facing and A, pick up and k 16 sts evenly along right side edge of border, knit next 179 sts, pick up and k 16 sts evenly along rem side of border—211 sts. Knit 1 row. Bind off knitwise.

Finishing
Sew side borders to side edges of blanket. Sew top/bottom borders to blanket.
Weave in ends. Block to finished measurements. ■

Gauge
20 sts and 28 rows to 4"/10cm over St st using size 6 (4mm) needles.
Take time to check gauge.

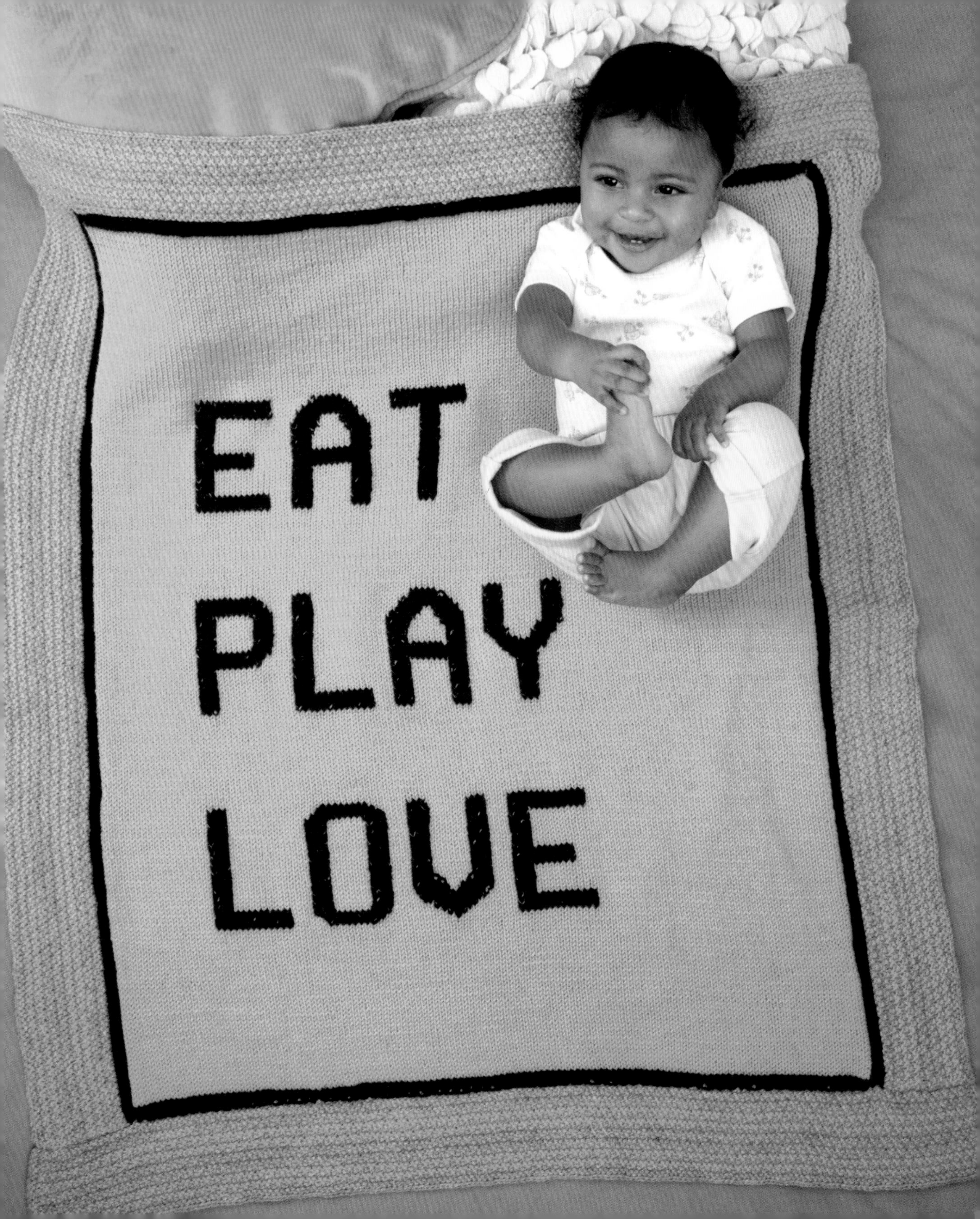
EAT
PLAY
LOVE

36

Eat Play Love

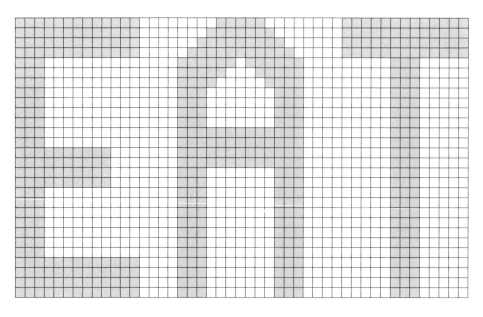

Color Key

☐ MC

▨ B

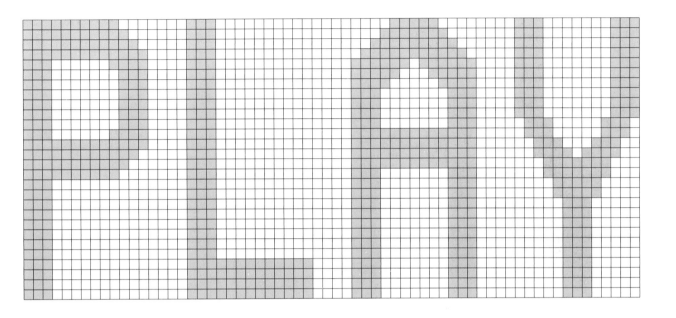

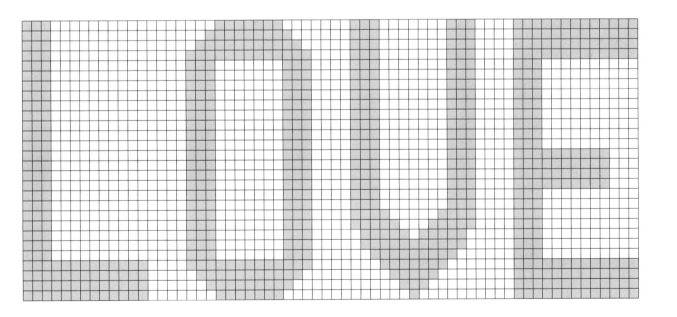

37

Good Vibrations

Stripes of rich, velvety color radiate from the center of this dramatic design.

DESIGNED BY IRINA POLUDNENKO

Knitted Measurements
Approx 31"/78.5cm square

Materials
■ 2 3½oz/100g hanks (each approx 128yd/117m) of Cascade Yarns *128 Superwash* (superwash merino) each in #1960 pacific (B) and #1910 summer sky heather (C)

■ 1 hank each in #1965 dark plum (A), #1947 amethyst heather (D), #1980 aster (E), and #1948 mystic purple (F)

■ One pair size 10 (6mm) needles *or size to obtain gauge*

■ Two size 10 (6mm) circular needles, 24"/60cm and 16"/40cm long

■ One set (5) size 10 (6mm) double-pointed needles (dpns)

■ Stitch markers

Note
Blanket is worked by knitting the triangle pattern border in 4 strips. Then, once border is seamed, sts for the inner square are picked up and knit and decreased to the center.

Blanket
BORDER STRIP
With straight needles and A, cast on 26 sts.
Work 1 outer edge triangle as foll:
Row 1 (RS) Sl 1, k to last 3 sts, k2tog, p1.
Row 2 Sl 1, k to last st, p1.
Row 3 With B, sl 1, k to last 3 sts, k2tog, p1.
Row 4 With B, sl 1, k to last st, p1.
Rep rows 1–4 until 3 sts rem.
K3tog. Cut yarn.
With RS facing and A, pick up and k 26 sts along short side of last triangle.
Knit one row.
Work 1 inner row triangle as foll:
Next row (RS) With C, Sl 1, k2tog, k to last st, p1.
Next row With C, sl 1, k to last st, p1.
Next row With A, Sl 1, k2tog, k to last st, p1.
Next row With A, sl 1 k to last st, p1.
Rep last 4 rows until 3 sts rem. K3tog. Cut C.
With RS facing and A, pick up and k 26 sts along short side of last triangle.
Knit one row.
Work 1 outer edge triangle.
Cont to work inner and outer edge triangles until there are 5 triangles in border strip 1.

BORDER STRIP 2 (3, 4)
Work as for border strip 1, using D (E, F) instead of A.
Sew the four strips tog to form a square by sewing the cast-on edges of each strip to the short edge of the next.

INNER SQUARE
With longer circular needle and A, [pick up and k 70 sts along inner edge of border, place marker] 4 times—280 sts.
Work in garter st stripe pat as foll:
Rnd 1 With A, [k2tog, k to 2 sts before next marker, k2tog, sl marker] 4 times.
Rnd 2 With A, purl.
Rnd 3 With B, [k2tog, k to 2 sts before next marker, k2tog, sl marker] 4 times.
Rnd 4 With B, purl.
Rep rnds 1–4 three times more, for 8 stripes. Cut yarn, join D.
Cont in garter st stripe pat in colors as foll: 8 stripes in D and C, 8 stripes in F and C, 4 stripes with A and B.
Cut B, leaving long tail, and thread tail through rem 4 sts.

Finishing
Weave in ends. Block lightly to finished measurements. ■

Gauge
15 sts and 30 rows to 4"/10cm over garter st using size 10 (6mm) needles.
Take time to check gauge.

Block and Tassel

Vibrant orange at the border and in the tassels makes this spirited throw sing.

DESIGNED BY GALINA CARROLL

Knitted Measurements
Approx 22" x 24"/56cm x 61cm

Materials
■ 2 3½oz/100g balls (each approx 220yd/201m) Cascade Yarns *220 Superwash* (superwash wool) each in #1960 pacific (MC) and #864 Christmas green (A)

■ 1 ball in #907 tangerine heather (B)

■ One pair size 8 (5mm) needles *or size to obtain gauge*

■ Size I/9 (5.5mm) crochet hook

Note
When changing colors, twist yarns on WS to prevent holes.

Blanket
Using cable cast-on, with A cast on 48 sts, with MC cast on 48 sts—96 sts.
Row 1 (RS) With MC, k48; with A, p48.
Row 2 With A, k48; with MC, p48.
Rep last 2 rows 8 times more, end with a WS row.
Row 19 With B, k48; with MC, k48.
Row 20 With MC, p48; with B, k48.
Row 21 With B, p48; with MC, k48.
Rep last 2 rows 7 times more, then rep row 20 once more.
Row 37 With MC, k48; with A, k48.
Rep rows 2–37 twice more, then rows 2–36 once, end with a WS row. Bind off in pat.

Finishing
Weave in ends. Block lightly.

EDGING
Rnd 1 (RS) With crochet hook and B, join with a sl st into any corner, *1 sc into every other row/st along side of blanket to corner st; 2 sc in corner st; rep from * 3 times more. Join with a sl st to first sc. Do not turn.

Rnd 2 Ch 1, *work 1 sc in each st to corner, work 2 sc into corner st; rep from * 3 times more. Join with a sl st to first sc.
Rnd 3 Repeat rnd 2. Fasten off.

TASSELS
Make 4 tassels in each A and B, each with a finished length of 2½"/6.5cm.

TASSEL TIES
Using 2 strands of yarn held together, make 4 twisted cords in each A and B, approx. 4"/10cm in length. Attach tassel to one end of twisted cord.
Tie 1 A and 1 B tassel tie to each corner of blanket, as shown in photograph. ■

Gauge
18 sts and 26 rows to 4"/10cm over St st using size 8 (5mm) needles.
Take time to check gauge.

Picture-Perfect Plaid

Country colors and a traditional plaid pattern add a bit of casual comfort to the nursery.

DESIGNED BY THERESA SCHABES

Knitted Measurements
Approx 31" x 41"/78.5cm x 104cm

Materials
- 4 3½oz/100g hanks (each approx 128yd/117m) Cascade Yarns *128 Superwash* (superwash merino) in #821 daffodil (A)
- 2 hanks each in #820 lemon (B) and #822 pumpkin (D)
- 1 hank each in #855 burgundy (C) and #817 ecru (E)
- Size 10 (6mm) circular needle, 32"/80cm long, *or size to obtain gauge*
- Size J/10 (6mm) crochet hook

Notes
1) Circular needle is used to accommodate large number of sts—do not join.
2) Wind separate balls of yarn for each block—do not carry yarn across back of work. Twist yarn when changing colors to eliminate holes.
3) Vertical stripes are worked with crochet hook after body of blanket is completed.

Blanket
With A, cast on 98 sts using crochet cast-on.

Row 1 (RS) With A, k17; *with B, k16; with A, k16; rep from * once more, with B, k17.
Row 2 (WS) With B, p17; *with A, p16; with B, p16; rep from * once more, with A, p17.
Rows 3–12 Rep last 2 rows 5 times more.
Row 13 (RS) With C, knit. Slide sts to other end of needle, ready to work a RS row.
Row 14 (RS) Rep row 1.
Row 15 (WS) Rep row 2.
Rows 16–25 Rep last 2 rows 5 times more. Slide sts to other end of needle, ready to work a WS row.
Row 26 (WS) With A, p17; *with D, p16; with A, p16; rep from * once more, with D, p17.
Row 27 (RS) With D, k17; *with A, k16; with D, k16; rep from * once more, with A, k17.
Rows 28–37 Rep last 2 rows 5 times more. Slide sts to other end of needle, ready to work a RS row.
Row 38 (RS) With E, knit.
Row 39 (WS) Rep row 26.
Row 40 (RS) Rep row 27.
Rows 41–50 Rep last 2 rows 5 times more. Slide sts to other end of needle, ready to work a RS row.
Rep rows 1–50 three times more.
Bind off.

VERTICAL STRIPES
With crochet hook and E, beg at lower edge and working in the ladder between the 9th and 10th sts of first column of A and D blocks, work a column of slip stitches to top edge: With RS facing, hold yarn on WS of work, insert crochet hook from RS to WS below first ladder rung and draw up a lp to RS, *insert hook below next ladder, draw up a lp and pull through lp on hook; repeat from * to top edge. Fasten off. Rep for remaining A and D columns, working between the 8th and 9th sts.
With crochet hook and C, work a line of slip stitches in the ladder between the 8th and 9th sts of first column of A and B blocks. Rep for rem A and B columns.

EDGING
With crochet hook and A, work a row of sc around blanket, working into every st on top and bottom edges and into every 3rd row on side edges, securing any yarn ends.
Next rnd *Sc in each sc to corner, 2 sc in next sc; rep from * around. Rep this rnd twice more. Fasten off.

Finishing
Block lightly to measurements. ■

Gauge
14 sts and 21 rows to 4"/10cm over St st using size 10 (6mm) needle. *Take time to check gauge.*

Hearts, Kisses, & Hugs

Nothing could say "I love you" more than this precious pattern of Xs, Os, and hearts. Perfect for your little valentine!

DESIGNED BY E. J. SLAYTON

Finished Measurements
Approx 28" x 35"/71cm x 88.5cm

Materials
- 5 3½oz/100g hanks (each approx 128 yd/117m) of Cascade Yarns *128 Superwash* (superwash merino) in #1964 cerise
- Size 9 (5.5mm) circular needle, 24"/61cm or longer, *or size to obtain gauge*
- Stitch markers
- Cable needle

Stitch Glossary
4-st RC Sl 2 sts to cn and hold in back, k2, k2 from cn.
4-st LC Sl 2 sts to cn and hold in front, k2, k2 from cn.
M1 Insert LH needle from back to front under the strand between last st worked and next st on the LH needle. Knit into the front loop to twist the st.

Hugs & Kisses Cable Pattern
(panel of 10 sts)
Row 1 (RS) P1, 4-st RC, 4-st LC, p1.

Row 2 and all WS rows K1, p8, k1.
Row 3 P1, k8, p1.
Rows 5–8 Rep rows 1–4.
Row 9 P1, 4-st LC, 4-st RC, p1.
Row 11 Rep row 3.
Rows 13–16 Rep rows 9–12.
Rep rows 1–16 for hugs & kisses cable pat.

Hearts Pattern
(panel of 15 sts)
Row 1 (RS) K15.
Row 2 P15.
Row 3 K7, p1, k7.
Row 4 P6, k3, p6.
Row 5 K5, p2, k1, p2, k5.
Row 6 P4, k2, p3, k2, p4.
Row 7 K3, p2, k5, p2, k3.
Row 8 P2, k2, p7, k2, p2.
Row 9 K2, p2, k3, p1, k3, p2, k2.
Row 10 P2, k2, p2, k3, p2, k2, p2.
Row 11 K3, p4, k1, p4, k3.
Row 12 P4, k2, p3, k2, p4.
Rows 13–16 Rep rows 1 and 2 twice.
Rep rows 1–16 for hearts pat.

Blanket
Cast on 92 sts. Beg with a WS row and sl first st purlwise every row throughout, knit 5 rows, end with a WS row.
Inc row (RS) Sl 1, k4, pm; p1, [k1, M1] 4

times, p1, pm (cable—10 sts); *k4, M1, k5, M1, k4, pm (hearts—15 sts); p1, [k1, M1] 4 times, p1, pm; rep from * 3 more times, end k5—120 sts.
Next row (WS) Sl 1, k3, p1; k1, p8, k1; *p15; k1, p8, k1; rep from * 3 times more, end p1, k4. Slip markers as needed.
Pat row 1 (RS) Sl 1, k4; work row 1 of hugs & kisses cable pat, then *work row 1 of hearts pat, then work row 1 of hugs & kisses cable pat again. Rep from * 3 times more; end k5.
Keeping 5 edge sts each side as established on last 2 rows, cont to work pats in this way to row 16, then rep rows 1–16 seven times more, then rows 1–14 once more.
Dec row (RS) Sl 1, k4; p1, ssk twice, k2tog twice, p1; [k4, k2tog, k3, ssk, k4; p1, ssk twice, k2tog twice, p1] 4 times; k5, dropping markers—92 sts.
Cont to slip first st, knit 5 rows. Bind off all sts purlwise on next RS row.

Finishing
Weave in all ends. Block lightly to measurements. ■

Gauge
13 sts and 18 rows to 4"/10cm over heart pat st (blocked) using size 9 (5.5mm) circular needle.
Take time to check gauge.

Night Owl

What a hoot! An oversize owl keeps watch over little ones snug in their cribs.

DESIGNED BY LINDA MEDINA

Knitted Measurements
Approx 28" x 30"/71cm x 76cm

Materials
- 3 3½oz/100g balls (each approx 220yd/201m) Cascade Yarns *220 Superwash* (superwash wool) in #847 caribbean (MC)
- 1 ball each in #858 dark ginger (A), #841 moss (B), #876 sandalwood (C), #1920 pumpkin spice (D), and #878 lazy maize (E)
- Size 7 (4.5mm) circular needle, 32"/80cm long, *or size to obtain gauge*

Notes
1) Blanket is worked back and forth in rows. Circular needle is used to accommodate large number of sts—do not join.
2) When changing colors, twist yarns on WS to prevent holes and carry yarn not in use loosely across back of work.
3) Garter stitch borders are not shown on chart.
4) Chart is broken into two sections, A and B, which are numbered continuously. Work from the bottom to the top of Chart A, then continue with the bottom row of Chart B.

Basketweave Pattern
Row 1 (RS) Knit.
Row 2 Purl.
Row 3 K1, *p2, k2, rep from * to 1 st before border, p1.
Rows 4, 6, and 8 K the knit sts and p the purl sts.
Row 5 Knit.
Row 7 P1, *k2, p2, rep from * to 1 st before border, k1.
Rep rows 1–8 for basketweave pat.

Slip Stitch Pattern
(over multiple of 6 sts plus 5)
Row 1 (RS) With D, p4, *wyif sl 3 sts purlwise, p3; rep from * to last st, p1.
Row 2 With D, k4, *wyib sl 3 sts purlwise, k3; rep from * to last st, k1.
Row 3 With E, knit.
Rows 4 and 6 With E, purl.
Row 5 With E, k5, *insert point of RH needle under the 2 strands of D, knit the next st, bringing the new st under the 2 strands of D, k5; rep from * to end of row.
Row 7 With D, P1, *wyif sl 3 sts purlwise, p3; rep from * to last 4 sts, wyif sl 3 sts purlwise, p1.
Row 8 With D, K1, *wyib sl 3 sts purlwise, k3; rep from * to last 4 sts, wyib sl 3 sts purlwise, k1.

Gauge
18 sts and 28 rows to 4"/10cm over slip stitch pattern using size 7 (4.5mm) needles.
Take time to check gauge.

Night Owl

Row 9 With E, knit.
Row 10 With E, purl.
Row 11 With E, K2, *insert point of RH needle under the 2 strands of D, knit the next st, bringing the new st under the 2 strands of D, k5; rep from * to last 3 sts, insert point of RH needle under the 2 strands of D, knit the next st, bringing the new st under the 2 strands of D, k2.
Row 12 With E, purl.
Rep rows 1–12 for slip stitch pat.

Blanket

With MC, cast on 142 sts.
Work 9 rows in garter st (knit every row), end with a WS row.
Work basketweave pat for 22 rows.

BEG CHART

Next row (RS) K6, work row 1 of Chart A over next 130 sts, k6.
Next row K6, work row 2 of Chart A over next 130 sts.
Keeping first and last 6 sts in garter st, cont as now established, working appropriate row of chart, to end of chart B (row 142).
Work basketweave pat for 44 rows.
Work 9 rows in garter st, end with a RS row. Bind off all sts knitwise.

Finishing

Block to finished measurements.

EMBROIDERY

Eyelashes Using photo as a guide, with D, embroider eyelashes around each eye using running stitch.
Topknot Using photo as a guide, with C, embroider topknot feathers at top of head using running stitch. ∎

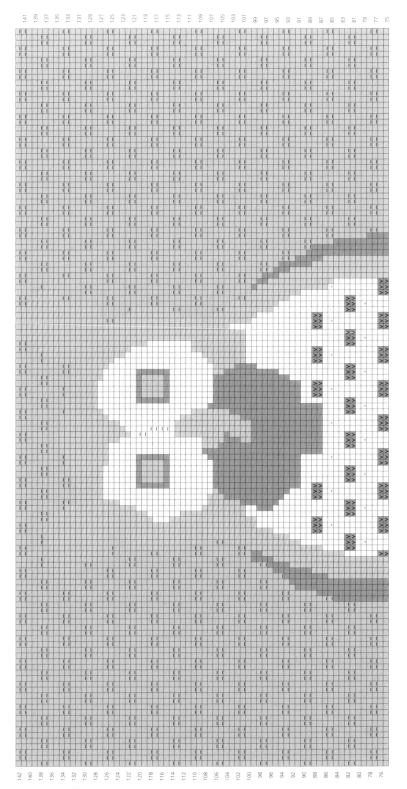

Color & Stitch Key

- ☐ MC, K on RS, P on WS
- ⊟ MC, P on rS, K on WS
- ■ A, K on RS, P on WS
- ▨ B, K on RS, P on WS
- ⊟ B, P on RS, K on WS
- ☐ C, K on RS, P on WS
- ⊟ C, P on RS, K on WS
- ▨ D, k on RS, p on WS
- ⊟ D, p on RS, k on WS
- ☑ D, wyif sl 1 on RS, wyib sl 1 on WS
- ☐ E, k on RS, p on WS
- ⊟ E, p on RS, p on WS
- ⊡ E, insert point of RH needle under the 2 strands of D, knit the next st, bringing the new st under the 2 strands of D

Fringe Element

Brighten up a simple pattern of chunky rectangles with fun shades of pink and purple and fringed edges.

DESIGNED BY GALINA CARROLL

Knitted Measurements
Approx 24" x 25½"/61cm x 64.5cm, excluding fringe

Materials
■ 1 3½oz/100g ball (each approx 220yd/200m) of Cascade Yarns *220 Superwash* (superwash wool) each in #902 soft pink (A), #881 then there's mauve (B), and #903 flamingo pink (C)

■ One pair size 7 (4.5mm) needles *or size to obtain gauge*

■ Size I/9 (5.5mm) crochet hook

■ Bobbins (optional)

Seed Stitch
(over even number of sts)
Row 1 (RS) *K1, p1; rep from * across.
Rep row 1 for seed st.

Note
When changing colors, bring new color up from under old to avoid gaps. Wind yarn onto separate bobbins or small balls for easier handling.

Blanket
With B, cast on 30 sts; with A, cast on 30 sts; with C, cast on 30 sts; with A, cast on 30 sts. Begin chart, working each tier for 25 rows and working all A sections in St st (k on RS, p on WS), all B sections in seed st, and all C sections in garter st (k every row). Work a total of 7 tiers (175 rows). Bind off in pat.

Finishing
Block lightly. With crochet hook and B, work 1 rnd of sc around outside edge, ending with a multiple of 3 sts.
Next rnd *Ch 5, skip next 2 sc, sc in next sc; rep from * around. Join. Fasten off. Cut B into 6"/15cm lengths. In groups of 3, join as fringe in every other ch-5 lp along shorter ends as shown. ■

Gauge
21 sts and 29 rows to 4"/10cm over St st using size 7 (4.5mm) needles.
Take time to check gauge.

Fringe Element

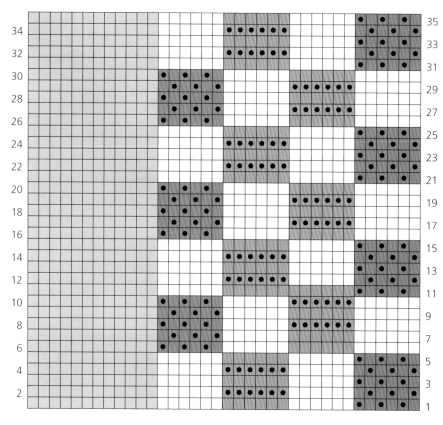

Stitch Key

☐ Knit (RS: knit stitch, WS: purl stitch)

⊡ Purl (RS: purl stitch, WS: knit stitch)

▨ No stitch

Counting Sheep

Sleepy babies will love to cuddle with the sleepy sheep that graces this adorable throw.

DESIGNED BY JACQUELINE VAN DILLEN

Knitted Measurements
Approx 29½" x 39½"/75cm x 100cm

Materials
■ 4 3½oz/100g hanks (each approx 128yd/117m) of Cascade Yarns *128 Superwash* (superwash merino) each in #875 feather grey (A) and #1926 doeskin heather (B)

■ 2 hanks in #817 ecru (C)

■ 1 3½ oz/100g ball (each approx 220yd/201m) of Cascade Yarns *220 Superwash* (superwash wool) in #862 walnut heather (D)

■ One size 10 (6mm) circular needle, 40"/100cm long, *or size to obtain gauge*

■ Size H/8 (5mm) crochet hook

■ 1yd/1m fabric for lining

■ Yarn needle for embroidering face

■ Sewing needle and thread for lining

■ Stitch markers

Note
Work body of blanket in rows; pick up border work in the round. Crochet sheep separately and sew on.

Loop Stitch
Row 1 Sc in each st across.
Row 2 Ch 1, *insert the hook next sc, wrap the yarn over your finger, making a lp, draw the yarn from the far side of the lp through the st (2 lps on hook), yo hook and draw through both lps to complete the sc; rep from * in each sc across.
Repeat these 2 rows for loop st.

Blanket
With A, cast on 91 sts. Work in St st until piece measures 34"/86.5cm from beg. Bind off.

BORDER
With B and RS facing, pick up and k 131 sts along each side edge and 93 sts each along the bound-off and cast-on edges—448 sts. Place marker for beg of rnd and in each corner st. Sl marker each rnd and move corner st markers up each rnd. Knit one rnd.
Next (inc) rnd [Knit to the marked st, yo, k1, yo] 4 times.
Rep inc rnd every other rnd 3 times more. Purl 1 rnd.
Next (dec) rnd [Knit to 1 st before marked st] 4 times.
Rep dec row every other row 4 times, then knit 1 rnd. Bind off.

Sheep
LEGS (MAKE 4)
With C and crochet hook, ch 26. Dc in 3rd ch from hook (first 2 ch count as dc), dc in each dc across to last ch, work 5 dc in last ch, place marker in center st of this group; working into other side of foundation ch, work 1 dc in each ch. Turn.
Next row Ch 2 (counts as dc), 1 dc in each dc to marked st, work 3 dc in marked st, 1 dc in each dc to end. Fasten off.

EARS (MAKE 2)
Ch 8. Work as for leg.

Gauges
14 sts and 18 rows to 4"/10cm using size 10 (6mm) needle and A.
14 dc to 4"/10cm using size H/8 (5mm) crochet hook and C. *Take time to check gauges.*

121

Counting Sheep

HEAD
Ch 19. Dc in 3rd chain from the hook, dc in each ch to last ch, work 5 dc in last ch, place marker in center st of this group; working into other side of foundation ch, work 1 dc in each ch. Turn.

Next row Ch 2 (counts as dc), dc in each dc to 1 st before marked st, work 3 dc in this st, dc in marked st, remove marker, 3 dc in next dc, dc in each dc to end. Turn. Place markers in center st of each 3dc group.

Next row Ch 2 (counts as dc), 1 dc in each dc to marked st, 3 dc in marked st,

1 dc in each dc to next marked st, 3 dc in marked st, dc in each dc to end. Fasten off.

BODY
With C, ch 8. Work 1 sc in 3rd ch from hook, work sc in each ch to end, ch 6, turn.

Next row 1 sc in 2nd ch from hook, 1 sc in next 3 sts, row 2 of loop st to end, ch 10, turn.

Next row 1 sc in 2nd ch from hook, 1 sc to end of row, turn.
Beg chart:

Set-up row (WS) Work in loop st over 19 sts, ch 9.
Beg with row 1, cont to work in this way, working incs and decs as indicated on chart.
When body is complete, work 1 row of sc, then row 2 of loop st around entire body.

Finishing
With D, using photo as guide, embroider face on sheep's head.
Sew the sheep pieces to the blanket, using photo as guide. Sew lining fabric to WS of blanket. Fold the edges of the border over the lining along the purl ridge and sew to WS.
With D, crochet a line of slip st crochet along the edges of the body of the blanket alongside the border.
Weave in ends; block lightly to measurements. ■

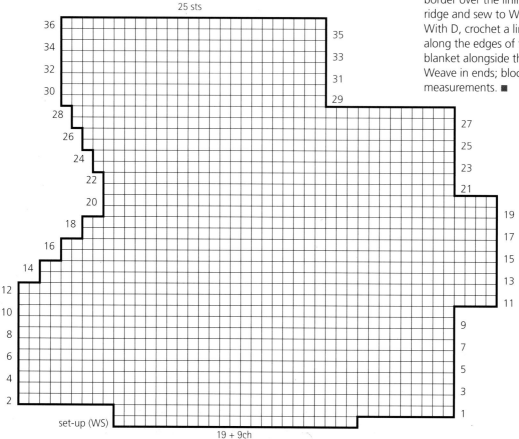

Pinstripe Perfection

What's black and white and striped all over? This versatile throw that will go with any décor.

DESIGNED BY RUTHIE NUSSBAUM

Knitted Measurements
Approx 30"/76cm square

Materials
- 2 3½oz/100g balls (each approx 220yd/200m) Cascade Yarns *220 Superwash* (superwash wool) each in #871 white (A) and #1913 jet (B)
- 1 ball in #886 citron (C)
- Size 8 (5mm) circular needle, 24"/60cm long, *or size to obtain gauge*
- Two size 7 (4.5mm) double-pointed needles (dpns)

Stripe Pattern
With A, k 1 row, p 1 row.
With B, k 1 row, p 1 row.
Rep these 4 rows for stripe pat.

Blanket
With circular needle and A, cast on 139 sts.
Row 1 With A, knit.
Row 2 With A, purl.
Row 3 With B, kfb, k to last st, kfb—2 sts inc'd.
Row 4 With B, purl.
Working in stripe pat, rep last 2 rows twice more—145 sts.
Cont in stripe pat until piece measures 29"/73.5cm from beg, end with a WS row. Maintaining stripe pat, work as foll:
Next row (RS) Ssk, k to last 2 sts, k2tog—2 sts dec'd.
Next row (WS) Purl.
Rep last 2 rows twice more—139 sts.
Bind off.

Finishing
I-CORD EDGING
With dpns and waste yarn, cast on 4 sts using a provisional cast-on. With RS of blanket facing and C, *k3, sl 1 purlwise, yo, pick up and k 1 st from lower edge of blanket, pass slipped st and yo over last st. Without turning, slide sts back to the opposite end of needle to work next row from RS. Pull yarn tightly from the end of row. Rep from *, working around edge of blanket. When edging is complete, place sts from provisional I-cord cast-on on dpns and graft to final row.
Weave in all ends and block lightly to measurements. ■

Gauge
19 sts and 29 rows to 4"/10cm over St st using size 8 (5mm) circular needle.
Take time to check gauge.

The Birds and the Bees

Birds and bees alternate with bars in a sweet and loving knitted lullaby.

DESIGNED BY JEANNIE CHIN

Knitted Measurements
Approx 28" x 33"/71cm x 84cm

Materials
- 2 3½oz/100g balls (each approx 220yd/201m) Cascade Yarns *220 Superwash* (superwash wool) each in #817 aran (MC) and #1917 vinci (A)
- 1 ball each in #876 sandalwood (B) and #821 daffodil (C)
- Size 8 (5mm) circular needle, 32"/80cm long, *or size to obtain gauge.*
- 1 yd/1m of coordinating fabric (for backing)
- Sewing needle and thread

Notes
1) Blanket is worked back and forth in rows. Circular needle is used to accommodate large number of sts—do not join.
2) When changing colors, twist yarns on WS to prevent holes in work.

Moss Stitch
(over an odd number of sts)
Rows 1 and 4 K1, *p1, k1; rep from * to end.
Rows 2 and 3 P1, *k1, p1; rep from * to end.
Rep rows 1–4 for moss st.

Blanket
BOTTOM EDGING
With A, cast on 125 sts. Work 14 rows in moss st, end with a WS row. Break A and join MC.

BEG CHART PAT
Next row (RS) Beg chart on row 1, work first 31 sts of chart, work 26-st rep three times, work last 16 sts of chart.
Cont as now established until 56-row repeat has been worked 3 times, then rows 1–42 once, end with a WS row. Break MC and join A.

TOP EDGING
Next row (RS) Knit.
Work 14 rows in moss st, end with a RS row. Bind off all sts in pat.

Finishing
SIDE BORDERS
With right side facing and A, pick up and k 173 sts evenly along side edge of blanket. Work 14 rows in moss st, end with a RS row. Bind off all sts in pat. Rep for opposite edge.
Weave in ends. Block to finished measurements.

LINING
Cut lining fabric 25"/63.5cm wide by 30"/76cm long. Fold to WS ½"/1.5cm seam allowance along all edges. Place fabric on ironing board wrong side up, fold over seam allowances and press. Mark center of each side of fabric lining with a pin. Mark center of each side of knitted blanket (excluding borders) with a stitch marker. Lay lining on table, wrong side up, and place knitted piece on top, right side up. Pin together, matching center points and corners on each side, and ensure that the blanket is sitting straight on the lining. Slip stitch blanket to lining. ■

Gauge
21 sts and 30 rows to 4"/10cm over chart pattern using size 8 (5mm) needles.
Take time to check gauge.

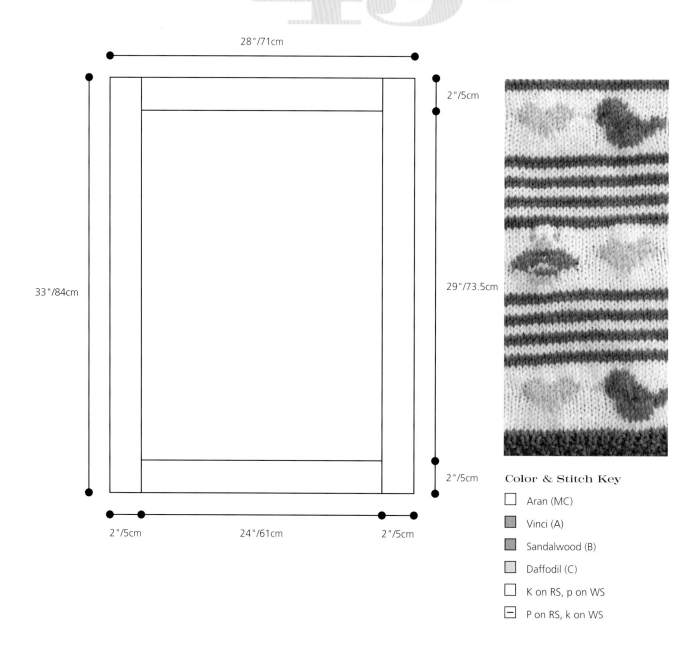

28"/71cm

2"/5cm

33"/84cm

29"/73.5cm

2"/5cm

2"/5cm 24"/61cm 2"/5cm

Color & Stitch Key

☐ Aran (MC)

▨ Vinci (A)

▩ Sandalwood (B)

☐ Daffodil (C)

☐ K on RS, p on WS

⊟ P on RS, k on WS

46

Diamonds in the Rough

Pops of fuschia and an unconventional shape add a touch of the unexpected to warm autumn hues.

DESIGNED BY JACQUELINE VAN DILLEN

◀■☐◗

Knitted Measurements
Approx 29½" x 41½"/75cm x 105cm

Materials
■ 2 3½oz/100g balls (each approx 220yd/201m) of Cascade Yarns *220 Superwash* (superwash wool) each in #823 burnt orange (A), #877 golden (B), and #826 tangerine (C)

■ 1 ball each in #903 flamingo pink (D), #837 berry pink (E), and #825 orange (F)

■ One pair size 8 (5mm) needles *or size to obtain gauge*

■ 4 stitch markers in 2 different colors (2 in each color)

Note
Blanket is worked in garter stitch strips, which are sewn together. Markers are placed in 4 squares, 2 in strip 6 and 1 each in strips 5 and 7, to aid in matching strips for finishing.

Strips
Cast on 20 sts with first color, knit 42 rows in each designated color, bind off with last color.

Blanket
Work strips in the following colors:
Strip 1 A.
Strip 2 B, C, D.
Strip 3 E, F, E, A, B.
Strip 4 A, B, A, B, C, E, C.
Strip 5 D, F, E, D, F, A, B, D (place first color marker in this square), A.
Strip 6 C (place 2nd color marker in this square), E, A, B, E, C, F, E (place first color marker in this square), F.
Strip 7 F, D (place 2nd color marker in this square), A, C, D, A, D, B, A.
Strip 8 B, C, B, A, F, E, C.
Strip 9 A, E, F, D, B.
Strip 10 C, B, A.
Strip 11 D.

Finishing
With RS facing and cast-on edges at the RH side, center strip 1 on the upper edge of strip 2 and sew tog. Rep for strips 2–5. Then rep for strips 7–11. Sew strip 6 to strips 5 and 7, beg at the squares with the matching markers.
Weave in ends. Block lightly to measurements. ■

Gauge
18 sts and 36 rows to 4"/10cm over garter st using size 8 (5mm) needles.
Take time to check gauge.

Not Your Granny's Square

A neutral throw becomes youthful and fun with a border of brightly colored granny squares.

DESIGNED BY WILMA PEERS

Knitted Measurements
Approx 31" x 37.5"/79cm x 95cm
Granny squares: 3"/7.5cm square

Materials
■ 3 3½oz/100g skeins (each approx 220yd/200m) of Cascade *220 Superwash* (superwash wool) in #875 feather grey (MC)

■ 1 skein each #849 dark aqua, #821 daffodil, #842 light iris, #834 strawberry pink, #802 green apple

■ One size 10 (6mm) circular needle 32" long, *or size to obtain gauge*

■ Size D/3 (3.25mm) crochet hook

Notes
1) The granny squares are worked into the back of crochet st of previous row. It will provide a right side, stitches showing off as chain stitches between rows.
2) Change color at discretion, but keep rnds 3 and 4 the same color for a cleaner look.

Granny Squares
Ch 5 sts. Sl st through the first st to form a lp.
Rnd 1 Ch 3, 2 dc into loop, ch 3, (3 dc, ch 3) 3 times, sl st into top of ch 3.
Rnd 2 Ch 3, 2 dc tbl, *(2 dc, ch 3, 2 dc) into ch 3 sp, 3 dc tbl; rep from * twice, (2 dc, ch 3, 2 dc) into ch 3 sp, sl st into top of ch 3.
Rnd 3 Ch 3, 4 dc tbl, *(2 dc, ch 3, 2 dc) into ch 3 sp, 7 dc tbl; rep from * twice, (2 dc, ch 3, 2 dc) into ch 3 sp, sl st into top of ch 3.
Rnd 4 Ch 3, 4 dc tbl, *(2 dc, ch 3, 2 dc) into ch 3 sp, 11 dc tbl; rep from * twice, (2 dc, ch 3, 2 dc) into ch 3 sp, dc 2 tbl, sl st into top of ch 3.
Fasten off.

Seed Stitch
(over odd number of sts)
Rnd 1 K1, P1, repeat to end of row, k1.
Rep rnd 1 for seed st.

Blanket
Make 7 granny squares and sew them together. Pick up stitches into the back lp of each of the granny squares. Work in seed st until blanket measures 36"/91.5cm. Bind off in pat.
Work 12 granny squares for each long side of the blanket and another set of 7 squares for the other short end of the blanket, for a total of 31 granny squares.

Finishing
Tie in all ends. Steam border strips. Sew first granny square of long border strip to bottom granny square, then attach to the seed st panel, leaving one granny square to turn the corner. Sew remaining granny square together with the first granny square of short strip. Attach short strip to seed st panel. Sew first and last granny square of second long strip to short granny squares and the remainder to the seed st panel. Weave in ends and block lightly to measurements. ■

Gauge
20 sts and 28 rows to 4"/10cm over seed st using size 10 (6mm) circular needle.
Take time to check gauge.

Ribbon Candy

Garter stitch and eyelets combine for a sweet candy-inspired effect.

DESIGNED BY KATHARINE MALLER

Knitted Measurements
Approx 36" x 46"/91.5cm x 117cm

Materials
- 4 3½oz/100g balls (each approx 220yd/200m) Cascade Yarns *220 Superwash* (superwash wool) in #903 flamingo pink (A)
- 3 balls in #817 aran (B)
- 1 ball in #809 really red (C)
- Size 8 (5mm) circular needle, 40"/100cm long, *or size to obtain gauge*
- Size G/6 (4mm) crochet hook

Eyelet Stripe Pattern
(over an even number of sts)
Rows 1–2 With B, knit.
Row 3 With B, *k2tog, yo; rep from * to end.
Rows 4–5 With B, knit.
Row 6 Rep row 3.
Rows 7–8 With B, knit.
Rows 9–22 With A, knit.
Rep rows 1–22 for eyelet stripe pat.

Note
Circular needle is used to accommodate large number of sts—do not join.

Blanket
With A, cast on 200 sts.
Knit 14 rows.
Work rows 1–22 of eyelet stripe pat 13 times.
Bind off.

Finishing
EDGING
Row 1 With WS facing, crochet hook, and C, work 1 hdc for every 2 rows.
Row 2 Hdc in each hdc.
Row 3 Rev-sc in each hdc. Fasten off.
Rep for second side edge.
Block lightly to measurements. ■

Gauge
18 sts and 35 rows to 4"/10cm over garter st using size 8 (5mm) needle.
Take time to check gauge.

Bundled Up

A new arrival will snuggle happily in this plush bunting with scalloped edges
and playful tassels at head and feet.

DESIGNED BY LORI STEINBERG

Knitted Measurements
Width unfolded at widest point
23"/58.5cm
Length from point of hood to bottom
point 27"/ 68.5cm

Materials
■ 3 1¾oz/50g balls (each approx
137yd/125m) Cascade Yarns *220
Superwash Sport* (superwash wool) in
#1973 seafoam heather

■ Size 7 (4.5mm) circular needle,
24"/60cm long, *or size to obtain gauge*

■ H/8 (5mm) crochet hook

■ Stitch markers

■ Velcro® dots

■ Sewing needle and thread to
match yarn

Note
Blanket is worked back and forth in rows.
Circular needle is used to accommodate
large number of sts—do not join.

Drop Stitch Pattern
(over a multiple of 3 sts plus 2)
Rows 1, 3, and 5 (RS) K2, *p1, k2; rep
from * to end.
Rows 2 and 4 P2, *k1, p2; rep from * to
end.
Row 6 P2, drop next st from LH needle,
insert tip of RH needle in st 5 rows below
and knit, catching the 4 loose strands
behind the new st, p2.
Rep rows 1–6 for drop stitch pat.

Blanket
Cast on 101 sts. Work in drop st pat
until piece measures approx 14"/35.5cm
from beg.
Place marker at end of this row.

SHAPE SHOULDERS
Cont in pat, bind off 2 sts at beg of next
30 rows—41 sts.
Work even until piece measures
8"/20.5cm from marker, end with
a WS row.
Next row Work 18 sts, k2tog, work to
end of row.
Divide sts on 2 needles with RS tog, and
bind off using 3-needle bind-off method.

Finishing
Fold lower edge so that corners meet at
center, and sew seam to form pouch.

EDGING
With crochet hook, beg above pouch,
ch 1, work 133 sc along side edge of
blanket, around hood, to above pouch
on opposite side.
Next row Ch 1, sc in first sc, *sk 1 sc,
5dc in next sc, sk 1 sc, 1 sc in next sc; rep
from * to end.
Fasten off.
Make 2 tassels and sew one to top of
hood and one to point of pouch. Weave
in ends and block lightly to
measurements.

VELCRO FASTENERS
Using photo as guide, swaddle baby and
mark places to add fasteners. Sew
fasteners in place so they will be hidden
when baby is swaddled. ■

Gauge
18 sts and 26 rows to 4" over drop stitch pat using size 7 (4.5mm) needle.
Take time to check gauge.

Silver and Gold

A simple variation on seed stitch creates a uniquely beautiful texture, in a modern and versatile color combo.

DESIGNED BY MICHÈLE FANDEL BONNER

Knitted Measurements
Approx 23" x 33"/58.5cm x 84cm

Materials
■ 4 3½oz/100g hanks (each approx 128yd/117m) Cascade Yarns *128 Superwash* (superwash merino) in #1946 silver (A)

■ 1 hank in #821 daffodil (B)

■ Size 10 (6mm) circular needle, 24"/60cm long, *or size to obtain gauge*

■ Two size 10 (6mm) double-pointed needles (dpns)

Diagonal Seed Stitch
(over multiple of 4 sts)
Row 1 (RS) *K3, p1; rep from * to end.
Row 2 (WS) P1, *k1, p3; rep from * to last 3 sts, k1, p2.
Row 3 K1, *p1, k3; rep from * to last 3 sts, p1, k2.
Row 4 *P3, k1; rep from * to end.
Rep rows 1–4 for diagonal seed st.

Blanket
With circular needle and waste yarn, cast on 80 sts using a provisional cast-on. With A, beg diagonal seed stitch pat and work until piece measures 32"/81cm. Cut yarn, leaving sts on needle.

I-CORD EDGING
Note When working along side edges, pick up 3 sts for every 4 rows.
With dpns and waste yarn, cast on 4 sts using a provisional cast-on. With RS of blanket facing and B, k4, k first blanket st on circular needle, *sl these 5 sts to circular needle, K3, SKP, k next blanket st; rep from * across top edge.
K 1 row of I-cord to ease around corner by sliding sts back to opposite end of dpns to work next row from RS, pull yarn tightly from end of row and K4. Pick up and k 1 st from the corner. Slide sts back to opposite end of dpns.
Beg at top of side edge, *k3, SKP, pick up and k 1 st from side edge. Without turning, slide sts back to the opposite end of needle to work next row from RS. Rep from * along side edge. Work corner as before.
Remove waste yarn and place lower edge sts on circular needle, work as for top edge. Work corner as before. Work second side edge as for first side edge. When edging is complete, place sts from provisional I-cord cast-on on dpns and graft to final row.

Finishing
Weave in all ends. Block lightly to measurements. ■

Gauge
14 sts and 25 rows to 4"/10cm over diagonal seed st using size 10 (6mm) circular needle.
Take time to check gauge.

Diamonds and Purls

Individual knitted squares are sewn together to form diamonds in this stylish graphic blanket.

DESIGNED BY DEBBIE O'NEILL

Knitted Measurements
Approx 29"x 38"/73.5cm x 96.5cm
(38"/96.5cm square)
Instructions are given for small-size
blanket. Changes for larger size are given
in parentheses.

Materials
■ 4 (5) 3½oz/100g balls (each approx
220yd/201m) of Cascade Yarns *220
Superwash* (superwash wool) each in
#1973 seafoam heather (A) and #1946
silver grey (B)

■ One pair size 7 (4.5mm) needles *or size
to obtain gauge*

■ Size 7 (4.5mm) circular needle,
36"/91cm long

Blanket
With straight needles and A,
cast on 35 sts.

FIRST TRIANGLE
Set-up row (WS) Knit.
Row 1 (RS) With A, knit to last 2 sts,
k2tog—2 sts dec.
Row 2 Knit.
Rep rows 1 and 2 until 2 sts remain.
Next row K2tog, break yarn and pull
through loop.

SECOND AND SUBSEQUENT
TRIANGLES
With RS facing and B, pick up and k 35
sts along one short edge of triangle.
Work triangle as above. Cont until 4
triangles have been worked, alternating
between color A and color B (2 triangles
of each color in square).

Repeat to make a total of 12
(16) squares.

Finishing
Complete each square by seaming the
first and last triangles tog. Arrange
completed squares as shown in diagram.
Seam the squares into strips, then seam
the strips into the final blanket.

BORDERS
With circular needle and B, RS facing,
pick up and k 107 (140) sts along short
edge of blanket. Knit 1 row. Bind off
loosely, leaving last st live on needle.
Counting this as the first st, pick up and
k 140 sts along long edge. Knit 1 row,
bind off as before, leaving last st live.
Rep on rem sides.
Weave in ends and block lightly to
measurements. ■

Gauge
20 sts and 40 rows to 4"/10cm over garter st using size 7 (4.5mm) needles.
Take time to check gauge.

Diamonds and Purls

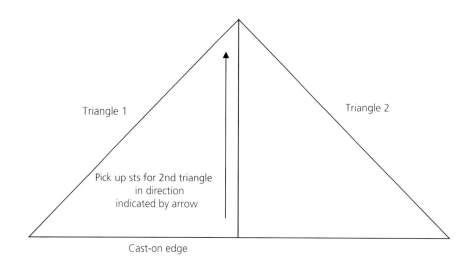

Triangle 1

Triangle 2

Pick up sts for 2nd triangle
in direction
indicated by arrow

Cast-on edge

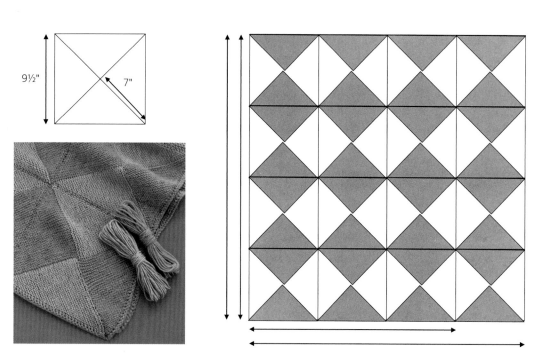

9½"

7"

Little Star

Put a twinkle in baby's eye with this lacy and graphic oversize star motif.

DESIGNED BY JACQUELINE VAN DILLEN

Knitted Measurements
31½" x 39½"/80cm x 100cm

Materials
■ 6 3½oz/100g hanks (each approx 128yd/117m) of Cascade Yarns *128 Superwash* (superwash merino) each in #817 ecru

■ Size 8 (5mm) circular needle, 36"/90cm long, *or size to obtain gauge*

■ One set (4) size 8 (5mm) double-pointed needles (dpns)

■ Size H/8 (5mm) crochet hook

■ Stitch marker

Stitch Glossary
M6 Insert LH needle from front to back, under the strand between the last st worked and the next st on the LH needle and [k1, p1] 3 times into this strand to make 6 sts.

Note
Blanket is worked in the round from the center out.

Blanket
With dpns, cast on 6 sts. Divide sts evenly among 3 needles. Join, taking care not to twist sts, and pm for beg of rnds.

Rnd 1 (inc) Inc 1 st in each st around—12 sts.
Rnd 2 and all even rnds K the knit sts and yos, and p the purl sts.
Rnd 3 [K1, yo, k1, yo, k1] 4 times around.
Rnd 5 [K1, p1, yo, k1, yo, p1, k1] 4 times around.
Rnd 7 [K1, p2, yo, k1, yo, p2, k1] 4 times around.
Rnd 9 [K1, p2, k1, yo, k1, yo, k1, p2, k1] 4 times around.
Rnd 11 [K1, p2, k2, yo, k1, yo, k2, p2, k1] 4 times around.
Rnd 13 [K1, p2, k3, yo, k1, yo, k3, p2, k1] 4 times around.
Rnd 15 [K1, p2, k4, yo, k1, yo, k4, p2, k1] 4 times around.
Rnd 17 [K1, p2, SKP, k7, k2tog, p2, k1, *k1, yo, k1, yo, k1; rep from * once more] 4 times around.
Rnd 19 [K1, p2, SKP, k5, k2tog, p2, k1 M6] 4 times around.
Rnd 21 [K1, p2, SKP, k3, k2tog, p2, k1, *k1, p1, yo, k1, yo, p1, k1; rep from * once more] 4 times around.
Rnd 23 [K1, p2, SKP, k1, k2tog, p2, k1, * k1, p2, yo, k1, yo, p2, k1; rep from * once more] 4 times around.
Rnd 25 [K1, p2, S2KP, p2, k1, *k1, p2, k1, yo, k1, yo, k1, p2, k1; rep from *

Gauge
15 sts and 34 rnds to 4"/10cm over St st using size 8 (5mm) circular needle.
Take time to check gauge.

Little Star

once more] 4 times around.

Rnd 27 [SKP, p3, k2tog, * k1, p2 ,k2, yo, k1, yo, k2, p2, k1; rep from * once more] 4 times around.

Rnd 29 [SKP, p1, k2tog; *k1, p2, k3, yo, k1, yo, k3, p2, k1; rep from * once more] 4 times around.

Rnd 31 [SK2P, *k1, p2, k4, yo, k1, yo, k4, p2, k1; rep from * once more] 4 times around.

Rnd 33 [P1, yo, k1, p2, SKP, k7, k2tog, p2, k1, M6] 4 times around.

Rnd 35 [P2, yo, k1, p2, SKP, k5, k2tog, p2, k1, * rep from * once more, k1, p2, SKP, k5, k2tog, p2, k1, yo, p1] 4 times around.

Rnd 37 [P3, yo, k1, p2, SKP, k3, k2tog, p2, k1, *k1, p1, yo, k1, yo, p1, k1; rep from * once more, k1, p2, SKP, k3, k2tog, p2, k1, yo, p2] 4 times around.

Rnd 39 [P4, yo, k1, p2, SKP, k1, k2tog, p2, k1, *k1, p2, yo, k1, yo, p2, k1; rep from * once more, k1, p2, SKP, k1, k2tog, p2, k1, yo, p3] 4 times around.

Rnd 41 [P5, yo, k1, p2, S2KP, p2, k1, *k1, p2, k1, yo, k1, yo, k1, p2, k1; rep from * once more, k1, p2, S2KP, p2, k1, yo, p4] 4 times around.

Rnd 43 [P6, yo, SKP, p3, k2tog, *k1, p2, k2, yo, k1, yo, k2, p2, k1; rep from * once more, SKP, p3, k2tog, yo, p5] 4 times around.

Rnd 45 [P7, yo, SKP, p1, k2tog, *k1, p2, k3, yo, k1, yo, k3, p2, k1; rep from * once more, SKP, p1, k2tog , yo, p6] 4 times around.

Rnd 47 [P8, yo, SK2P, k1, p2, k4, yo, k1, yo, k4, p2, k1 yo, k1, p2, k4, yo, k1, yo, k4, p2, k1 S2KP, yo, p7] 4 times around.

Rnd 49 [P9, yo, k2tog, k1, p2, SKP, k7,

k2tog, p2, k1, yo, inc 1 st in next st, yo, P9, yo, k2tog, k1, p2, SKP, k7, k2tog, p2, k1, k2tog, yo, p8] 4 times around.

Rnd 51 [P10, yo, k1, p2, SKP, k5, k2tog, p2, k1, yo, p1 yo, p2, yo, p1, yo, k1, p2, SKP, k5, k2tog, p2, k2tog, yo, p9] 4 times around.

Rnd 53 [P11, yo, k1, p2, SKP, k3, k2tog, p2, k1, yo, p3, yo, p2, yo, p3, yo, p10] 4 times around.

Rnd 55 [P12, yo, k1, p2, SKP, k1, k2tog, p2, k1, yo, p5, yo, p2, yo, p5, yo, p11] 4 times around.

Rnd 57 [P13, yo, k1, p2, SK2P, p2, k1, yo, p7, yo, p2, yo, p7, yo, p12] 4 times around.

Rnd 59 [P14, yo, SKP, p3, k2tog, yo, p9, yo, p2, yo, p9, yo, p13] 4 times around.

Rnd 61 [P15, yo, SKP, p1, k2tog, yo, p11, yo, p2, yo, p11, yo, p14] 4 times around.

Rnd 63 [P16, yo, S2KP, yo, p13, yo, pm, p2, yo, p13, yo, p15] 4 times around.

Next rnd Purl.

Next rnd [P to marker, yo, sl marker, p2, yo] 4 times around. Rep last 2 rnds 12 times more.

Bind off 3 sides. Work back and forth in rev St st on rem side for 6"/15cm more. Bind off.

Finishing

With crochet hook, work 3 rnds of sc around entire edge of blanket.

Next rnd [*1 sc in next sc, skip 3 sc, 7 dc in next sc, skip 3 sc; rep from * to corner st, work 9 dc, in corner st, skip 3 sc] 4 times, fasten off after last 9 dc cluster. Weave in ends. Block lightly to measurements. ∎

Mustachioed

Say goodbye to your stiff upper lip! These whimsical mustaches will
bring a smile to everyone's face.

DESIGNED BY CHRISTINA BEHNKE

Knitted Measurements
Approx 36" x 30"/91.5cm x 76cm

Materials
■ 5 3½oz/100g hanks (each approx
128yd/117m) of Cascade Yarns *128
Superwash* (superwash merino) in #1910
summer sky heather (MC)

■ 1 hank in #1913 jet (CC)

■ Size 10 (6mm) circular needle,
60"/150cm long, *or size to obtain gauge*

■ Size J/10 (6mm) crochet hook

Barber Pole Stitch
(over multiple of 6 sts)
Row 1 (RS) *K2, p3, k1; rep from * to
end.
Row 2 and all even (WS) rows Purl.
Row 3 *K1, p3, k2; rep from * to end.
Row 5 *P3, k3; rep from * to end.
Row 7 *P2, k3, p1; rep from * to end.
Row 9 *P1, k3, p2; rep from * to end.
Row 11 K3, p3; rep from * to end.
Rep rows 1–11 for barber pole st.

Blanket
LOWER BORDER
With MC, cast on 126 sts.
Rows 1–8 Work in barber pole st, ending
with a WS row.

BEGIN CENTER PANEL
Row 9 Work first 6 sts in barber pole st
as est, work in St st to last 6 sts, work to
end in barber pole st.
Rows 10–25 Work even as est.
Row 26 (WS) Work first 6 sts in barber
pole st, work 34 sts in St st, pm, work 46
sts in St st, pm, work 34 sts in St st, work
final 6 sts in barber pole st.

BEGIN HANDLEBAR CHART
Work 6 sts in barber pole st, work in St st

to marker, work row 1 of Handlebar
chart to second marker, work in St st to
last 6 sts, work in barber pole st to end.
Continue in this manner, working chart
between the two markers until chart is
complete.
Next (RS) row Work first 6 sts in barber
pole st; work in St st to last 6 sts, work to
end in barber pole st.
Work even for 19 more rows, ending
with a WS row.

BEGIN WALRUS CHART
Work 6 sts in barber pole st, work in St st
to marker, work row 1 of Walrus chart to
second marker, work in St st to last 6 sts,
work in barber pole st to end.
Continue in this manner, working Walrus
chart between markers, until chart is
complete.
Next (RS) row Work first 6 sts in barber
pole st; work in St st to last 6 sts, work to
end in barber pole st.
Work even for 19 more rows, ending
with a WS row.

Gauge
15 sts and 22 rows to 4"/10cm over St st using size 10 (6mm) circular needle.
Take time to check gauge.

Mustachioed

BEGIN BOULANGER CHART
Work 6 sts in barber pole st, work in St st to marker, work row 1 of Boulanger chart to second marker, work in St st to last 6 sts, work in barber pole st to end. Continue in this manner, working Boulanger chart between markers, until chart is complete.

Next (RS) row Work first 6 sts in barber pole st, work in St st to last 6 sts, work to end in barber pole st.

Work even for 19 more rows, ending with a WS row.

TOP BORDER
Work 8 rows in barber pole st, ending

with a WS row. Bind off knitwise on RS.

Finishing
Using crochet hook and CC, sc 96 sts along RS of blanket, sc 3 sts into top right corner st, sc 113 sts along top edge, sc 3 sts into top left corner st, sc 96 sts along left side edge, sc 3 sts into bottom left corner st, sc 113 sts along bottom edge, sc 3 sts into bottom right corner. Break yarn and sew through first sc st to join.

Weave in ends. Block lightly to measurements. ∎

BOULANGER

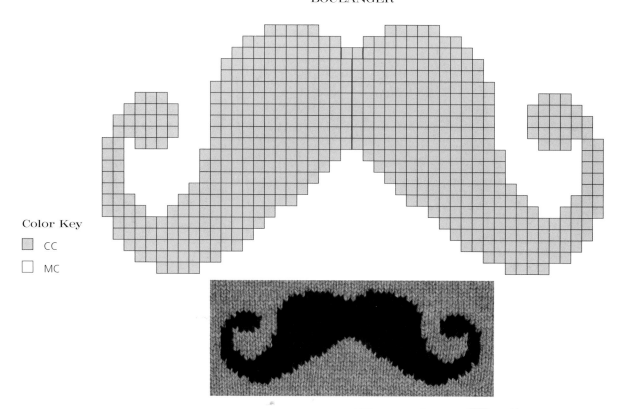

Color Key

▨ CC

☐ MC

WALRUS

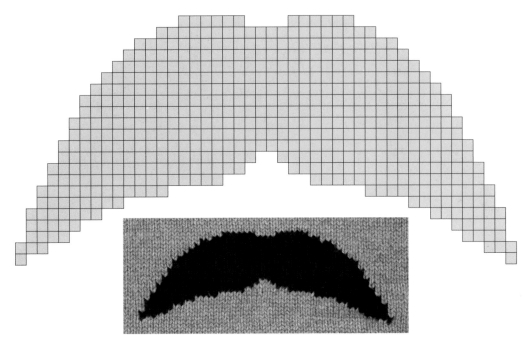

HANDLEBAR

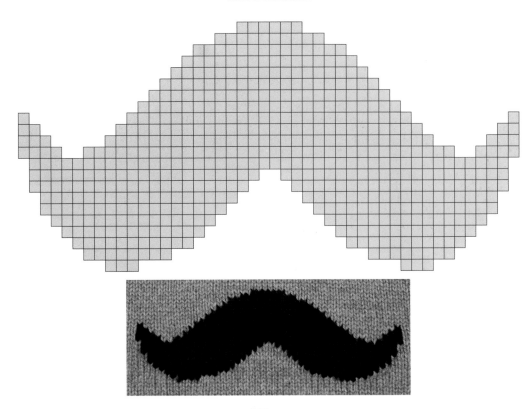

Cozy in Cables

An allover cable pattern and tasseled hood make a sweet bunting oh-so-special.

DESIGNED BY LORI STEINBERG

Knitted Measurements
Approx 24" x 29"/61cm x 73.7cm
unfolded after blocking

Materials
- 2 1¾oz/50g balls (each approx 137yd/125m) Cascade Yarns *220 Superwash Sport* (superwash merino) in #1940 peach
- Size 7 (4.5mm) circular needle, 24"/60cm long, *or size to obtain gauge*
- Cable needle (cn)
- Stitch markers
- Velcro® dot fasteners
- Sewing needle and thread to match yarn

Stitch Glossary
6-st LC Sl 3 sts to cn and hold to front, k3, k3 from cn.

Seed Stitch
(over an even number of sts)
Row 1 *K1, p1; rep from * around.
Row 2 K the purl sts and p the knit sts.
Rep row 2 for seed st.

Cable Check Pattern
(multiple of 12 sts plus 6)
Rows 1, 3, and 7 (RS) K6, *p6, k6; rep from * to end.

Row 2 and all WS rows K the knit sts and p the purl sts.
Row 5 6-st LC, *p6, 6-st LC; rep from * to end.
Rows 9, 11, and 15 P6, *k6, p6; rep from * to end.
Row 13 P6, *6-st LC, p6; rep from * to end.
Row 16 Rep row 2.
Rep rows 1–16 for cable check pat.

3-Needle Bind-off
1) Hold right sides of pieces together on two needles. Insert third needle knitwise into first st of each needle, and wrap yarn knitwise.
2) Knit these two sts together, and slip them off the needles. *Knit the next two sts together in the same manner.
3) Slip first st on 3rd needle over 2nd st and off needle. Rep from * in step 2 across row until all sts are bound off.

Note
Blanket is worked back and forth in rows. Circular needle is used to accommodate large number of sts—do not join.

Blanket
Cast on 42 sts. Work 8 rows in seed st.

BEG CABLE AND CHECK PAT
Work in cable and check pat for 2 16-row reps. Piece measures approx 6"/15cm from

beg. Place marker at both ends of this row.

SHAPE BODY
Cont in pat, inc 1 st each side every other row 36 times—114 sts. Work even until piece measures 15"/38cm from marker, end with a row 16 or 8. Place 2nd set of markers at both ends of this row.

SHAPE SHOULDERS
Bind off 12 sts at beg of next 6 rows—42 sts. Work even until piece measures 8"/20.5cm from 2nd set of markers. Work 7 rows in seed st. Divide sts on 2 needles with RS tog and bind off using 3-needle bind-off method.

Finishing
Block to measurements.

EDGING
Beg at lower edge with RS facing, pick up and k 156 sts to center of hood. **Next row (WS)** Work in seed st, working 3 sts into each of the 2 marked sts—160 sts. Work 8 rows even in seed st. Bind off in pat. Rep for other side of blanket. Make tassel and sew to top of hood.

VELCRO FASTENERS
Using photo as guide, mark places to add fasteners so they will be hidden when baby is swaddled; sew in place. ■

Gauge
20 sts and 32 rows over 4"/10cm in cable check pat after blocking, using size 7 (4.5mm) needle. *Take time to check gauge.*

Choo Choo

Eyelets form the shapes of engines, cars, and cabooses—waiting for the train has never been this much fun!

DESIGNED BY INGE SPUNGEN

Knitted Measurements
Approx 38"/96.5cm square

Materials
- 3 3½oz/100g hanks (each approx 128yd/117m) of Cascade Yarns *128 Superwash* (superwash merino) each in #897 baby denim (A) and #896 blue horizon (B)
- 2 hanks in #893 ruby (C)
- Size 9 (5.5mm) circular needle, 36"/91cm long, *or size to obtain gauge*
- Size I/9 crochet hook
- Waste yarn in contrasting color

Provisional Cast-on
With crochet hook and waste yarn, crochet a chain several stitches longer than the required number of stitches to be cast on. Fasten off. With knitting needle, pick up and knit the required number of stitches in the bumps of the chain, leaving a few empty loops at either end. When directed, "unzip" the stitches by undoing the end of the chain and pulling it out, placing the live sts on the needle.

Blanket
With B, cast on 127 sts using provisional cast-on method. Work in garter st (k every row) for 9 rows.
Set-up row (WS) K5, purl to last 5 sts, k5.
Row 1 (RS) K10, pm, work chart A, pm, work chart B, pm, work chart C, pm, k10.
Row 2 K5, purl to last 5 sts, k5.
Rep rows 1 and 2 until all rows of charts are complete, ending with a WS row. Change to C, work in garter st for 8 rows. Change to A, work in garter st for 34 rows. Change to C, work in garter st for 8 rows. Change to B, work in garter st for 34 rows. Change to C, work in garter st for 8 rows.

Change to A. Knit 1 row.
Set-up row (WS) K5, purl to last 5 sts, k5.
Row 1 (RS) K10, pm, work chart D, pm, work chart E, pm, work chart F, pm, k10.
Row 2 K5, purl to last 5 sts, k5.
Rep rows 1 and 2 until all rows of charts are complete, ending with a WS row. Work in garter st for 8 rows.

EDGING
Change to C and knit 1 row.
Continuing around edge of blanket, RS facing, pick up and k 130 sts along side of blanket. Remove waste yarn from cast-on edge, placing live sts on a second needle, then knit those sts. Pick up and k 130 sts on other side of blanket. Do not bind off.
Cast on 5 sts.
Row 1 Turn, *k4, knit next st tog with next st on edge of blanket.
Row 2 Turn, k5.
Rep rows 1 and 2 until all sts on first side of blanket have been used.

Gauge
14 sts and 20 rows to 4"/10cm over St st using size 9 (5.5mm) circular needle.
Take time to check gauge.

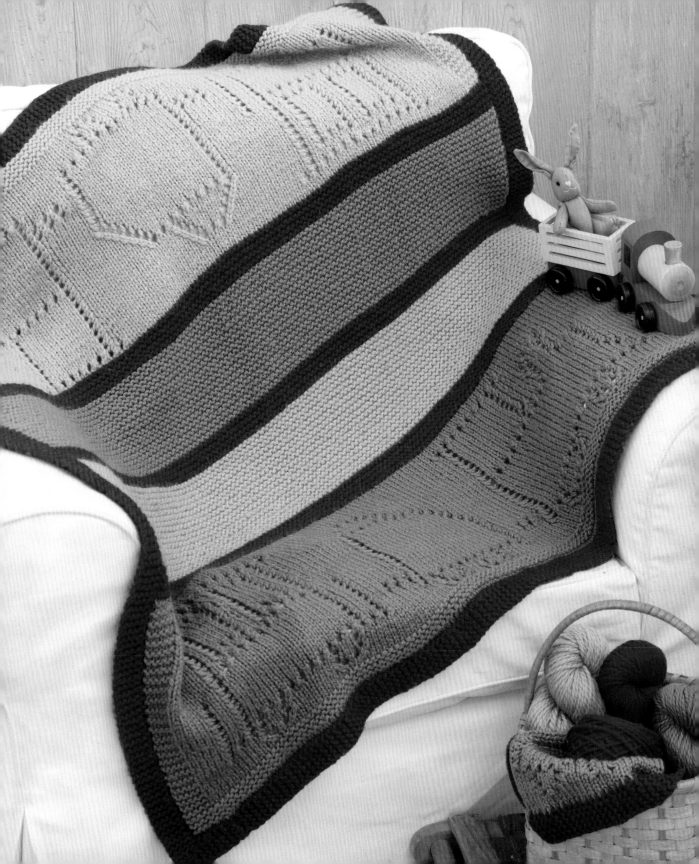

Choo Choo

CORNER

Row 1 K4, turn.
Row 2 K4, turn.
Row 3 K3, turn.
Row 4 K3, turn.
Row 5 K2, turn.
Row 6 K2, turn.
Row 7 K1, turn.
Row 8 K1, turn.
Row 9 K2, turn.
Row 10 K2, turn.
Row 11 K3, turn.
Row 12 K3, turn.
Row 13 K4, turn.
Row 14 K4, turn.**

Rep edging and corner between * and ** for remaining sides of blanket.

Finishing

Sew beg and ending edges of border tog. Weave in ends. Block lightly to measurements. ∎

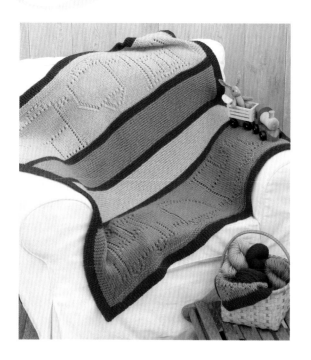

ENGINE CHART A

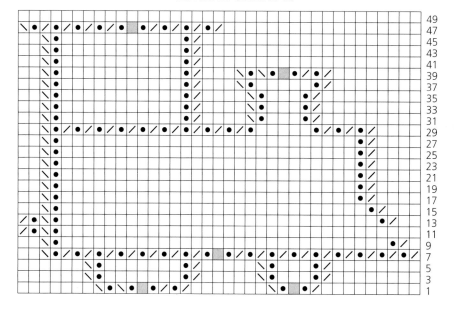

		49

Stitch Key

☐	Knit
●	Yarn over
╱	Knit 2 together
╲	Slip slip knit
▨	Knit

Choo Choo

COAL CAR CHART B

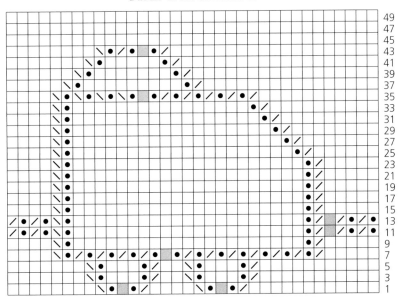

CABOOSE CHART C

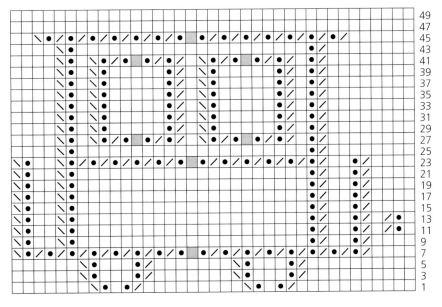

Choo Choo

CABOOSE CHART D

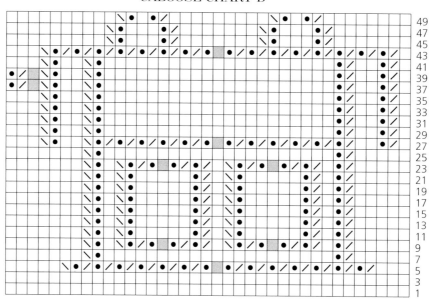

COAL CAR CHART E

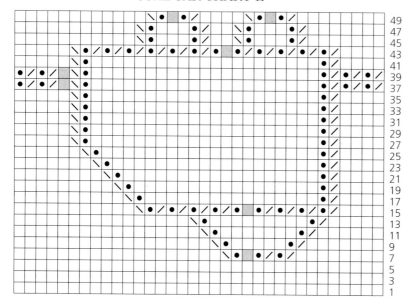

Choo Choo

ENGINE CHART F

Stitch Key

☐	Knit
●	Yarn over
╱	Knit 2 together
╲	Slip slip knit
▨	Knit

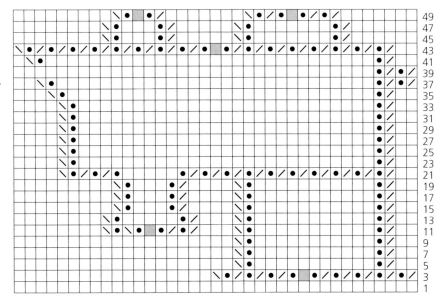

49
47
45
43
41
39
37
35
33
31
29
27
25
23
21
19
17
15
13
11
9
7
5
3
1

Heavenly Heathers

Switching colors on one strand at a time produces subtle marbled stripes
on a thick and cozy afghan that knits up quickly.

DESIGNED BY CAROL SULCOSKI

Knitted Measurements
Approx 30"/76cm square

Materials
■ 4 3½ oz/100g balls (each approx
220yd/201m) Cascade Yarns *220
Superwash* (superwash wool) in #874
ridge rock (MC)

■ 1 ball each in #886 citron (A), #891
misty olive (B), #841 moss (C), and #888
sage (D)

■ Size 11 (8mm) circular needle,
32"/80cm long, *or size to obtain gauge*

Notes
1) 2 strands of yarn are held together
throughout.
2) Blanket is worked back and forth in
rows. Circular needle is used to
accommodate large number of sts—do
not join.

Seed Stitch
(over an even number of sts)
Row 1 (RS) *K1, p1; rep from * to end.
Row 2 K the purl sts and p the knit sts.
Rep row 2 for seed st.

Blanket
With 2 strands of MC held together, cast
on 90 sts. Work 6 rows in seed st, end
with a WS row.
Next row (RS) Work first 4 sts in seed st
pat, knit to last 4 sts, work last 4 sts in
seed st pat.
Next row (WS) Work first 4 sts in seed st
pat, purl to last 4 sts, work last 4 sts in
seed st pat.
Rep last 2 rows for pat.
Cont in pat until piece measures
5"/12.5cm from beg, end with a WS
row. Break one strand of MC and join
one strand of A.

Cont in pat until piece measures
10"/25.5cm from beg, end with a WS
row. Break A and join one strand of B.
Cont in pat until piece measures
15"/38cm from beg, end with a WS row.
Break B and join one strand of C.
Cont in pat until piece measures
20"/51cm from beg, end with a WS row.
Break C and join one strand of D.
Cont in pat until piece measures
25"/63.5cm from beg, end with a WS
row. Break D and join one strand of MC.
Cont in pat until piece measures
29"/73.5cm from beg, end with a WS
row. Work 6 rows in seed st, end with a
WS row. Bind off all sts in pat.

Finishing
Weave in all ends. Block lightly to
measurements. ■

Gauge
12 sts and 17 rows to 4"/10cm over St st using 2 strands held together and size 11 (8mm) needle.
Take time to check gauge.

My Little Robot

The future is here, and it couldn't be cuter than this colorful space-age buddy.

DESIGNED BY VANESSA PUTT

Knitted Measurements
Approx 32"/81cm square

Materials
■ 2 3½oz/100g balls (each approx 220yd/200m) Cascade Yarns *220 Superwash* (superwash wool) in #809 really red (A)

■ 1 ball each in #812 turquoise (B), #817 aran (C), #821 daffodil (D), #816 gray (E)

■ Size 7 (4.5mm) circular needle, 24"/60cm long, *or size to obtain gauge*

Notes
1) Blanket is constructed log cabin style, beginning with center motif panel, and then picking up along edges for surrounding panels.
2) When changing colors, twist yarns on WS to prevent holes in work.
3) Blanket is knit back and forth in rows. Circular needle is used to accommodate large number of sts—do not join.

Blanket
ROBOT PANEL
With C, cast on 48 sts. Beg with RS row, work 6 rows in St st.

BEG CHART
Next row (RS) K6, work row 1 of chart over 36 sts, with C, k to end.
Cont to foll chart in this way, working sts on either side of chart in St st, through row 53. With C, work 6 rows more in St st. Bind off.

SIDE PANEL 1
With RS facing and A, beg at lower right corner, pick up and k 50 sts along right side edge of robot panel.
Row 1 (WS) P5, *k4, p4; rep from * to last 5 sts, k5.
Rep row 1 for 27 rows more. Bind off.

SIDE PANEL 2
With RS facing and A, beg at lower left corner of robot panel, pick up and k 48 sts along lower edge, 1 st in seam, and 21 sts along side edge of side panel 1—70 sts.
Row 1 (WS) P5, *k4, p4; rep from * to last 9 sts, k4, p5.
Row 2 (RS) K5, *p4, k4; rep from * to last 9 sts, p4, k5.
Rep last 2 rows, then rep row 1 once more.
Row 6 (RS) Purl.

Row 7 (WS) Knit.
Rows 8 and 9 Rep rows 6 and 7.
Rep rows 2–9 twice more, then rep rows 2–5 once more. Bind off.

SIDE PANEL 3
With RS facing and A, beg at top left corner of robot panel, pick up and k 50 sts along left side edge, 1 st in seam, and 19 along edge of side panel 2—70 sts.
Row 1 (WS) P5, *k4, p4, rep from * to last 9 sts, k4, p5.
Row 2 (RS) K5, *p4, k4; rep from * to last 9 sts, p4, k5.
Rep last 2 rows 13 times more. Bind off.

SIDE PANEL 4
With RS facing and A, beg at upper right corner, pick up and k 20 sts along side edge of side panel 1, 1 st in seam, 48 sts along top edge of robot panel, 1 st in seam, 20 sts along side edge of side panel 3—90 sts.
Beg with row 1, work as for side panel 2.

SIDE PANEL 5
With RS facing and B, beg at lower right corner, pick up and k 20 sts along side edge of side panel 2, 1 st in seam, 48 sts along edge of side panel 1, 1 st in seam, 20 sts along side edge of side panel—490 sts.

Gauge
18 sts and 26 rows to 4"/10cm over St st using size 7 (4.5mm) needle. *Take time to check gauge.*

My Little Robot

Row 1 (WS) K5, *p4, k4; rep from * to last 5 sts, p5.
Rows 2–5 Rep row 1.
Row 6 (RS) P5, *k4, p4; rep from * to last 5 sts, k5.
Rows 7–10 Rep row 6.
Rep rows 1–10 three times more. Bind off in pat.

SIDE PANEL 6

With RS facing and B, beg at lower left corner, pick up and k 20 sts along side edge of side panel 3, 1 st in seam, 68 sts along lower edge of side panel 2, 1 st in seam, 28 sts along side edge of side panel 5—118 sts.
*Work 5 rows in St st, 5 rows in rev St st (p on RS, k on WS); rep from * 3 times more. Bind off.

SIDE PANEL 7

With RS facing and B, beg at upper left corner, pick up and k 20 sts along side edge of side panel 4, 1 st in seam, 68 sts along edge of side panel 3, 1 st in seam, 28 sts along side edge of side panel 6—118 sts.
Row 1 (WS) K5, *p4, k4; rep from * to last 9 sts, p4, k5.
Row 2 (RS) P5, *k4, p4; rep from * to last 9 sts, k4, p5.
Rep last 2 rows, then rep row 1 once more.
Row 6 (RS) K5, *p4, k4; rep from * to last 9 sts, p4, k5.
Row 7 (WS) P5, *k4, p4; rep from * to last 9 sts, k4, p5.
Rows 8 and 9 Rep rows 6 and 7.
Row 10 (RS) Rep row 6.
Rep rows 1–10 three times more. Bind off in pat.

SIDE PANEL 8

With RS facing and B, beg at upper right corner, pick up and k 28 sts along side edge of side panel 5, 1 st in seam, 88 sts along upper edge of side panel 4, 1 st in seam, 28 sts along side edge of side panel 7—146 sts.
*Work 5 rows in St st, 5 rows in rev St st (p on RS, k on WS); rep from * 3 times more. Bind off.

Finishing
Block lightly. ∎

PLACEMENT DIAGRAM

8

4

| 7 | 3 | Robot | 1 | 5 |

2

6

57

My Little Robot

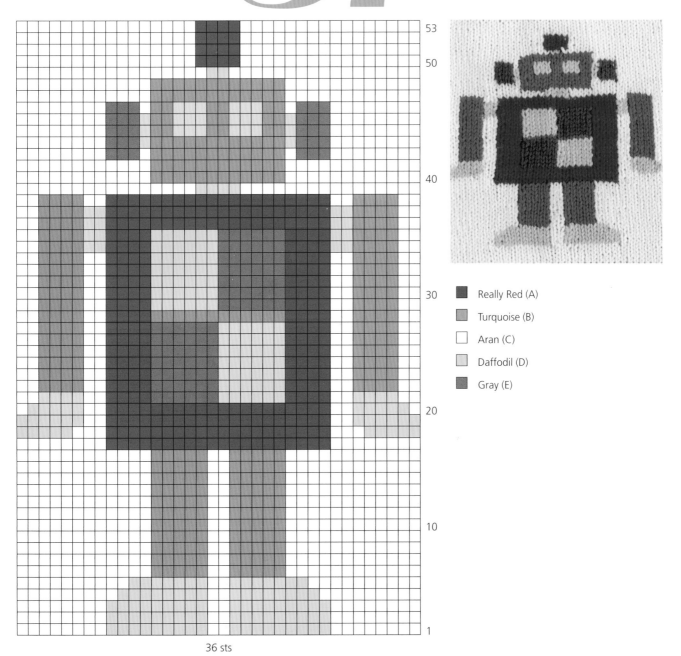

53

50

40

30

20

10

1

36 sts

■ Really Red (A)

■ Turquoise (B)

☐ Aran (C)

☐ Daffodil (D)

■ Gray (E)

Union Jack

Little Anglophiles will be ready for high tea in this stunning flag-inspired creation.

DESIGNED BY BRANDON MABLY

Knitted Measurements
Approx 33" x 26"/83.5cm x 66cm

Materials
■ 2 3½oz/100g balls (each approx 220yd/201m) of Cascade Yarns *220 Superwash* (superwash wool) each in #1925 cobalt heather (A), #1922 Christmas red (B), and #875 feather gray (C)

■ Size 7 (4.5mm) circular needle, 36"/90cm long, *or size to obtain gauge*

Blanket
SQUARE 1 (MAKE 2)
With A, cast on 84 sts. Reading chart from right to left for RS rows and left to right for WS rows, work rows 1–85 of chart. Bind off.

SQUARE 2 (MAKE 2)
With A, cast on 84 sts. Reading chart from left to right for RS rows and right to left for WS rows, work rows 1–85 of chart. Bind off.

Finishing
Arrange pieces with wide red stripes together at center to form Union Jack flag. Sew seams.

GARTER STITCH BORDER
Pick up and k 86 sts along one short side of blanket. Knit 10 rows. Bind off. Rep for other short side.
Pick up and k 178 sts along one long edge of blanket. Knit 10 rows. Bind off. Rep for other long edge.
Weave in ends. Block lightly to measurements. ■

Gauge
20 sts and 26 rows to 4"/10cm over St st using size 7 (4.5mm) circular needle.
Take time to check gauge.

Union Jack

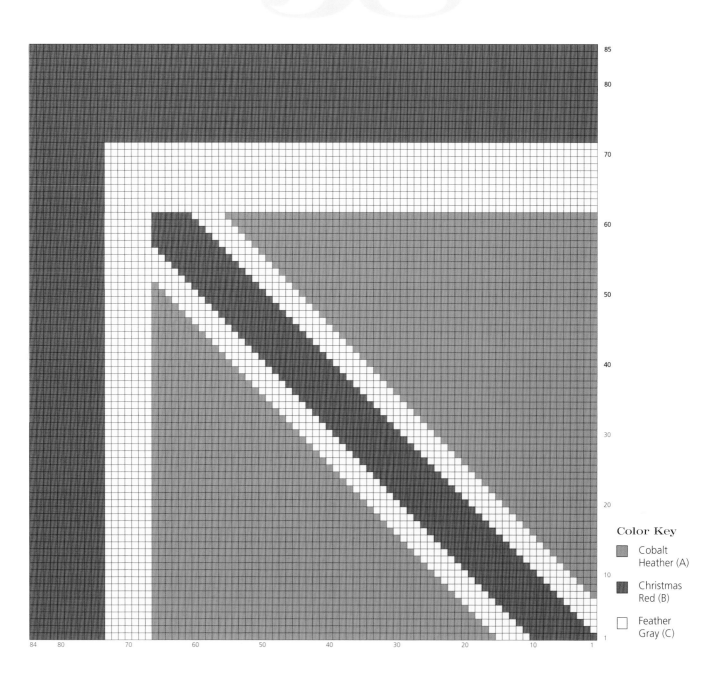

Color Key

- Cobalt Heather (A)
- Christmas Red (B)
- Feather Gray (C)

Shell Game

A troupe of whimsical three-dimensional turtles parades around a striped center.

DESIGNED BY AMY BAHRT

Knitted Measurements

Approx 28"/71cm square

Materials

■ 3 3½oz/100g balls (each approx 220yd/201m) of Cascade Yarns *220 Superwash* (superwash wool) in #810 teal (MC)

■ 2 balls in #845 denim (A)

■ 1 ball each in #802 green apple (B) and #842 light iris (C)

■ Size 7 (4.5mm) circular needle, 32"/80cm long, *or size to obtain gauge*

■ One set (5) size 7 (4.5mm) dpns

■ Size G/6 (4mm) crochet hook

Notes

1) Blanket is worked back and forth in rows. Circular needle is used to accommodate large number of sts—do not join.

2) When changing colors, twist yarns on WS to prevent holes in work.

Stripe Pattern

Work in St st as follows: *4 rows MC, 4 rows B; rep from * for stripe pat.

Blanket

With MC, cast on 138 sts. Work 8 rows in garter st, end with a WS row.

Next row (RS) With MC, k5; with A, k128; with MC, k5.

Next row With MC, k5; with A, p128; with MC, k5.

Rep last 2 rows 6 times more, end with a WS row.

BEG CHART A

Next row (RS) With MC, k5; with A, k31, [work row 1 of chart A over next 18 sts, with A, k8] twice, work row 1 of chart A over next 18 sts, with A, k27; with MC, k5.

Cont as established to end of chart A, end with a WS row.

Next row (RS) With MC, k5; with A, k128; with MC, k5.

Next row With MC, k5; with A, p128; with MC, k5.

Rep last 2 rows twice more, end with a WS row.

BEG CENTER STRIPE PANEL

**Next row (RS) With MC, k5; with A, k25; work stripe pat over next 78 sts, with A, k25; with MC, k5.

Next row With MC, k5; with A, p25; work stripe pat over next 78 sts, with A, p25; with MC, k5.

Rep last 2 rows once more, end with a WS row.

Gauge

20 sts and 26 rows to 4"/10cm over St st using size 7 (4.5mm) circular needle.

Take time to check gauge.

CHART A

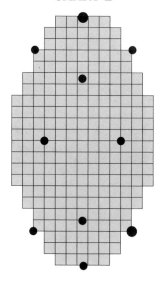

CHART B

Color Key

Teal (MC)

BEG CHART B

Next row (RS) With MC, k5; with A, k6; work row 1 of chart B over next 13 sts, with A, k6, work appropriate row of stripe pat over next 78 sts, with A, k6; work row 1 of chart B over next 13 sts, with A, k6; with MC, k5.
Cont as est to end of chart B, end with a RS row.**
Next row (WS) With MC, k5; with A, p25; work stripe pat over next 78 sts, with A, p25; with MC, k5.
Next row (RS) With MC, k5; with A, k25; work stripe pat over next 78 sts, with A, k25; with MC, k5.
Rep last 2 rows 5 times more, than first row once, end with a WS row.***
Repeat from ** to *** once more, then from ** to ** once, end with a RS row.
Next row (WS) With MC, k5; with A, p25; work following stripe pat over next 78 sts, with A, p25; with MC, k5.
Next row (RS) With MC, k5; with A, k25; work following stripe pat over next 78 sts, with A, k25; with MC, k5.
Rep last 2 rows 3 times more, then first row once, end with a WS row.
Next row (RS) With MC, k5; with A, k128; with MC, k5.
Next row With MC, k5; with A, p128; with MC, k5.
Rep last 2 rows twice more, end with a WS row.

BEG CHART A

Next row (RS) With MC, k5; with A, k31, [work row 1 of chart A over next 18 sts, with A, k8] twice, work row 1 of chart A over next 18 sts; with A, k27; with MC, k5.
Cont as established to end of chart A, end with a WS row.

Next row (RS) With MC, k5; with A, k128; with MC, k5.
Next row With MC, k5; with A, p128; with MC, k5.
Rep last 2 rows 6 times more, end with a WS row. Break A.
With MC, work 8 rows in garter st. Bind off all sts knitwise.

Finishing

Block to finished measurements.

TURTLE LEGS (MAKE 36)
With dpns and B, cast on 5 sts. *Knit one row. Without turning work, sl sts back to beg of row. Pull yarn tightly from end of row. Rep from * 8 times (I-cord measures approx. 1½"/4cm). Bind off knitwise. Attach legs as indicated on chart.

TURTLE HEAD (MAKE 12)
With dpns and B, cast on 6 sts. *Knit one row. Without turning work, sl sts back to beg of row. Pull yarn tightly from end of row. Rep from * 8 times (I-cord measures approx 1½"/4cm). Bind off knitwise. Attach heads as indicated on chart. Tack down top of head, leaving a slight bend as illustrated in photo.

TURTLE TAILS (MAKE 12)
With crochet hook and B, ch 8. Fasten off. Attach tails as indicated on chart, forming a small lp.

EMBROIDERY
With A, embroider a row of ch st around each turtle. With C, embroider French knots as indicated on chart. ∎

A New Leaf

A repeating leaf motif and a striped border tie together a plethora of pretty colors.

DESIGNED BY DEBBIE O'NEILL

■■■▣

Knitted Measurements

Approx 30" x 35"/76cm x 89cm
(35" x 41"/89cm x 104cm)
Instructions are written for small size.
Changes for larger size are in
parentheses.

Materials

■ 1 (2) 3½oz/100g balls (each approx
220yd/200m) of Cascade Yarns *220
Superwash* (superwash wool) each in
#836 pink ice (A), #838 rose petal (B),
#1967 wisteria (C), #840 iris (D), #1941
salmon (E), #831 rose (F)

■ 2 size 6 (4mm) circular needles,
47"/119.5cm long, *or size to obtain
gauge*

■ One set (5) size 6 (4mm) double-
pointed needles (dpns)

■ Stitch markers

Note

Border is knitted using circular needles.
Multiple needles are used to hold the
large number of sts.

SQUARE (MAKE 5 [7]
IN EACH COLOR)

With dpns, CO 8 sts, dividing sts evenly
over 4 needles. Join, taking care not to
twist sts. Place marker for beg of rnd.
Rnd 1 * K1, yo; rep from * to end of rnd.
Rnd 2 and all even rnds Knit.
Rnd 3 * K1, yo, k3, yo; rep from * to end
of rnd.
Rnd 5 * K1, yo, k5, yo; rep from * to
end of rnd.

Rnd 7 * K1, yo, k1, k2tog, yo, k1, yo,
ssk, k1, yo; rep from * to end of rnd.
Rnd 9 * K1, yo, k1, k2tog, k1, yo, k1, yo,
k1, ssk, k1, yo; rep from * to end of rnd.
Rnd 11 * K1, yo, k1, k2tog, k2, yo, k1,
yo, k2, ssk, k1, yo; rep from * to end of
rnd.
Rnd 13 * K1, yo, k1, k2tog, k3, yo, k1,
yo, k3, ssk, k1, yo; rep from * to end of
rnd.
Rnd 15 * K1, yo, k1, M1, ssk, k9, k2tog,
M1, k1, yo; rep from * to end of rnd.
Rnd 17 * K1, yo, k3, M1, ssk, k7, k2tog,
M1, k3, yo; rep from * to end of rnd.
Rnd 19 * K1, yo, k5, M1, ssk, k5, k2tog,
M1, k5, yo; rep from * to end of rnd.
Rnd 21 * K1, yo, k7, M1, ssk, k3, k2tog,
M1, k7, yo; rep from * to end of rnd.
Rnd 23 * K1, yo, k9, M1, ssk, k1, k2tog,
M1, k9, yo; rep from * to end of rnd.
Rnd 25 * K1, yo, k11, M1, sl 1, k2tog,
psso, M1, k11, yo; rep from * to end of
rnd—112 sts.
Bind off all sts loosely.

Steam-block the squares. Lay out the
completed squares in the desired pattern,
following the schematic. Seam the
squares into strips, then seam the strips
into the final blanket.

Gauges

20 sts and 24 rows to 4"/10cm over St st using size 6 (4mm) circular needle.
20 sts and 24 rows to 4"/10 cm in square pat st using size 6 (4mm) dpns. *Take time to check gauges.*

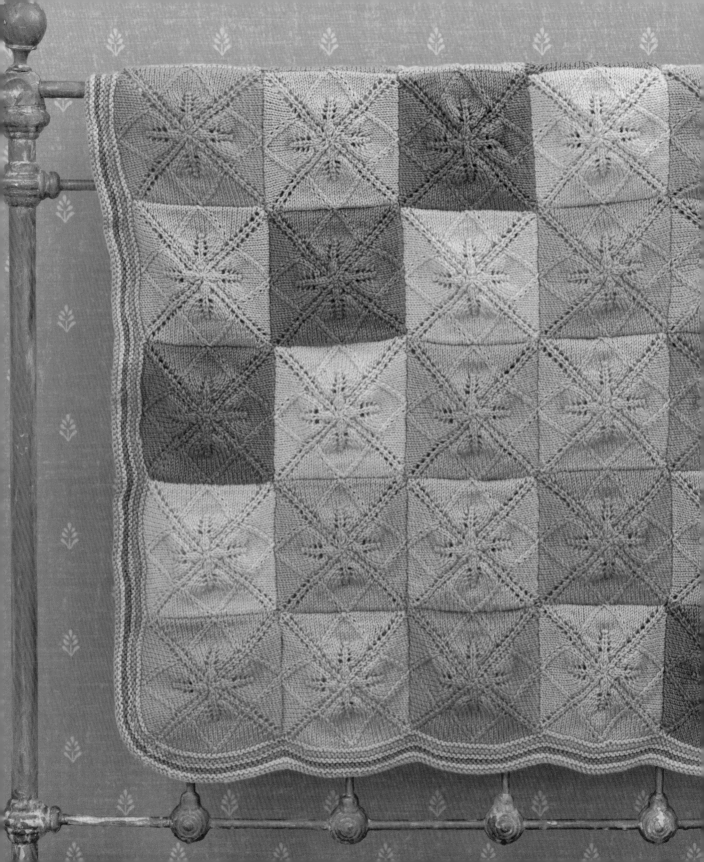

A New Leaf

BORDER

Using color A and circular needles, with RS facing, pick up and k 140 (168) sts along one short edge of the blanket, pm, pick up and k 1 st at the corner, pick up and k 168 (196) sts along the long edge, pm, pick up and k 1 st at the corner, pick up and k 140 (168) sts along the next short edge, pm, pick up and k 1 st at the corner, pick up and k 168 (196) sts along the final edge, pm, pick up and k 1 st at the corner—620 (732) sts. Purl one rnd. Break off yarn.

With B, knit to first marker, M1, sl marker, k1, M1, knit to second marker, M1, sl marker, k1, M1, knit to third marker, M1, sl marker, k1, M1, knit to final marker, M1, sl marker, k1, M1. Purl one rnd. Break off yarn.

Rep last 2 rnds with colors C, D, E, and F, adding 8 sts on each knit rnd. Bind off all sts loosely.

Finishing

Weave in all ends. Block lightly to measurements. ∎

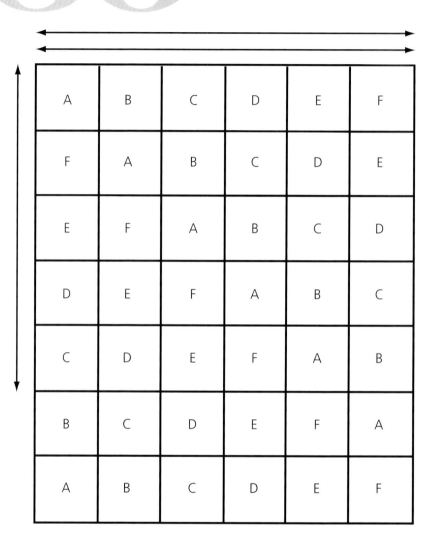

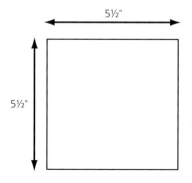

5½"

5½"

Little Lamb

Bonus project: a sweet and snuggly friend to cuddle with under the covers.

DESIGNED BY SUSAN B. ANDERSON

■■□□

Finished Measurements
Approx height 6"/15cm
Approx length 5"/13cm

Materials
■ 1 3½oz/100g ball (each approx 220yd/201m) of Cascade Yarns *220 Superwash* (superwash wool) each in #910A winter white (MC) and #1913 jet (A)

■ 1 ball in #902 soft pink

■ One set (4) size 6 (4mm) double-pointed needles (dpns) *or size to obtain gauge*

■ Stitch markers

■ Polyester stuffing

Loop Stitch (LS)
Knit the next st, leaving it on LH needle, bring yarn to front between the needles and wind it clockwise around your left thumb, bring yarn to back and k into the same st on LH needle, sl st off LH needle, sl 2 sts from RH needle back to LH needle and k them tog through back loops.

Gauge
22 sts and 32 rows to 4"/10cm over St st using size 6 (4mm) needles.
Take time to check gauge.

61 Little Lamb

Lamb
BOTTOM OF BODY
With MC, cast on 4 sts. Working back and forth in rows, proceed as follows:

Row 1 (RS) Kf&b, knit to last st, kf&b—6 sts.

Row 2 Pf&b, purl to last st, pf&b—8 sts.

Rep rows 1 and 2 once more—12 sts. Work even in St st until piece measures 2½"/6.5cm, end with a WS row.

Next (dec) row (RS) Ssk, knit to last 2 sts, k2tog—10 sts.

Next row P2tog, purl to last 2 sts, p2tog—8 sts.

Rep last 2 rows once more—4 sts.

BODY
Next row (RS) K4, turn work 90 degrees clockwise and pick up and k 38 sts evenly around bottom of body—42 sts.

Divide sts evenly onto 3 needles (14 sts per needle). Pm for beg of rnd.

Rnd 1 Knit.

Rnd 2 *K1, LS; rep from * to end of rnd.

Rnd 3 Knit.

Rnd 4 *LS, k1; rep from * to end of rn

Rep rnds 1–4 until body from pick-up row measures 2 1/2"/6.5cm, ending with rnd 2 or 4.

Next rnd *K5, k2tog; rep from * to end of rnd—36 sts.

Stuff the body with polyester stuffing. Place the first 18 sts on one dpn and the rem 18 sts on second dpn. Using kitchener st, close top of body.

HEAD
With MC, cast on 6 sts. Divide evenly among 3 needles (2 sts each needle). Join to work in rnds, being careful not to twist sts. Pm for beg of rnd.

Rnds 1, 3, 5, and 7 Knit.

Rnds 2 and 4 Kf&b in each st across—24 sts.

Rnd 6 [Kf&b, k6, kf&b] 3 times—30 sts.

Rnd 8 [Kf&b, k8, kf&b] 3 times—36 sts. Work a further 1"/2.5cm in St st. Break MC and join A.

FACE
Rnds 1, 3, 5, and 7 Knit.

Rnd 2 [Ssk, k8, k2tog] 3 times—30 sts.

Rnd 4 [Ssk, k6, k2tog] 3 times—24 sts.

Rnd 6 [Ssk, k4, k2tog] 3 times—18 sts.

Rnd 8 [Ssk, k2, k2tog] 3 times—12 sts.

Rnd 9 Knit.

Stuff head with polyester stuffing.

Next rnd [K1, k2tog, k1] 3 times—9 sts. Break yarn, leaving a long end. Thread end tightly through rem sts and fasten securely. Place the head facing to the side as shown in photo and whipstitch in place to body.

EARS (MAKE 2)
With MC, pick up and k 4 sts along the side of the sheep's head in a horizontal line. Work 10 rows in garter st (k every row).

Next row Ssk, k2tog—2 sts.

Next row K2tog. Fasten off.

Pinch the base of the ear together and secure with a couple of whipstitches. Sew a couple of sts into the head to hold the ear "down."

LEGS (MAKE 4)
With A, cast on 12 sts. Divide evenly among 3 needles (4 sts each needle). Join to work in rnds, being careful not to twist sts. Pm for beg of rnd. Work in St st rnds until leg measures 1½"/4cm.

Next rnd *K2, k2tog; rep from * to end—9 sts.

Break yarn, leaving a long end. Thread end tightly through rem sts and fasten securely.

Stuff leg with polyester stuffing. Whipstitch the leg to the bottom of the sheep's body, positioning the four legs so the sheep can stand.

EYES
With MC, using photo as a guide, embroider a small horizontal stitch to make the eye, then add a tiny vertical stitch in the center, catching the horizontal stitch and pulling it slightly upward.

NOSE
With C, using photo as a guide, embroider 2 straight stitches positioned between eyes to form a "V." ∎

index